Clever with Cakes

HOME COOKING

Clever with Cakes

BY
THE EDITORS OF TIME-LIFE BOOKS

TIME-LIFE/GEDDES & GROSSET

Contents

The Key to Better Eating 9
Almond-Apricot Fingers 10
Angel Cake Casket with Mango Filling 11
Apple and Date Cake 12
Apple Cake with Currants 13
Apricot and Pine-Nut Roll 14
Banana and Cardamom Cakes 15
Banana Layer Cake 16
Banana Tofu Cake 17
Banana Walnut Cake 18
Caraway Seed Sponge 19
Candied Fruit Cake Squares 20
Carrot and Walnut Cake 21
Chiffon Cake with Raspberry-Cream Filling 22
Chocolate Marble Cake 23

Cherry and Almond Sponge 24
Spiced Sherry Cake 24
Cinnamon Rock Cakes 26
Chocolate and Ginger Cheesecakes 27
Coffee Butterfly Cakes 28
Coffee Walnut Cake 29
Cool Caribbean Cake 30
Courgette Cake 32
Dundee Cake 33
Espresso Cakes 34
Fairy Cakes 35
Farmhouse Fruit Cake 36
Fig Cake Encased in Shortcrust 37

Frosted Orange Cake	38	Pistachio Battenburg Cake	51
Grapefruit Cake	39	Pumpkin Cake	52
Harvest Cake	40	Raisin and Ginger Buttermilk Cake	53
Iced Sponge Cakes	41	Saffron Fruit Cake	54
Lemon Curd Cakes	42	Semolina Fruit Cake	55
Madeleines	43	Simnel Cake	56
Orange and Lemon Ring Cake	44	Spiced Apricot Balmoral Cake	58
Parsnip and Orange Cake	45	Spiced Teacakes	59
Pear and Orange Upside-Down Cake	46	Strawberry Shortcake	60
Pear and Port Wine Cheesecake	47	Tropical Fruit Cake	61
Petal Ring Cakes	48	Vanilla Angel Cake	62
Pineapple Cake	49	Vinegar Cake	63
Pineapple Rondels	50	Black Cherry Chocolate Gateau	64

Clever with Cakes

To many, cakes seem the epitome of nutritional frivolity—mere concentrated sugar and fat. Yet for the sweet-toothed, life without the occasional feather-light sponge, moist fruit cake or chocolate-covered morsel would be much the poorer. The recipes in this volume are proof that cake can find a place in a healthy diet without overloading it with calories or sacrificing nutritional balance. A 2000-calorie daily diet can accommodate both a 175 calorie dessert and a 250-calorie snack, either of which might consist of some home-baked delight.

Above all, the cakes devised for this volume are ones in which fat—particularly saturated fat—is limited. The slices of temptation that give cakes a bad name are rich in butter and eggs and nuts, drowned in cream or chocolate. All should be consumed in moderation in a wholesome diet, since dairy products, chocolate and some nuts, notably coconut, are high in saturated fat and egg yolks are the main dietary source of cholesterol. A high level of cholesterol in the blood is strongly implicated in coronary heart disease, and blood cholesterol is raised by eating large quantities of saturated fat. Some experts believe that a diet high in cholesterol itself also helps to raise blood cholesterol.

Controlling saturated fat intake

To control the amounts of saturated fats and cholesterol in these cakes has challenged the recipe-creators' ingenuity, for the ingredients high in these undesirable fats play an important structural role. Butter and eggs make cakes moist, palatable and light.

One of the ways to cut down on saturated fat is to replace butter with a less saturated fat; polyunsaturated fats not only are not implicated in heart disease but actually seem to reduce blood cholesterol. The majority of the recipes in this volume call for polyunsaturated margarine rather than butter: many margarines, particularly the hard ones, contain nearly as much saturated fat as butter, but margarine made from sunflower oil, for instance, is predominantly polyunsaturated. The recipes in this book that use oil specify safflower, the most polyunsaturated available; if it is impossible to find, substitute sunflower, the next healthiest.

Many home-baking enthusiasts not only appreciate the health value of margarine but actually prefer it to butter. Soft margarines require less working than butter and give lighter results. On the other hand, butter confers an incomparable flavour.

The balance of health, flavour and texture can never be resolved for all time; it depends on the recipe and on each person's eating habits. Families that consume a lot of cake would be wise to cut down on butter—but if a slice of cake is a very rare treat, you may prefer to put flavour first. In most recipes, you can freely interchange margarine and butter, though a recipe that calls for butter but also contains a good deal of liquid may give too soft a result when polyunsaturated margarine is substituted. You cannot interchange oil with butter or margarine: the difference in density makes for different results and, unlike butter and margarine, oil will not incorporate air when beaten.

Butter has been limited in the cakes in this volume

not only because of the risk of heart disease but also for the sake of the calorie count. Weight for weight, fat contains more than double the calories of carbohydrate or protein, so any modest diminution in the butter content of a recipe will sharply reduce calories. Substituting margarine or oil for butter does nothing for the calorie count, because margarine is as high in calories as butter, and oil still higher. But the total fat content can be reduced by finding other ways of making the cake light and moist.

Fortunately, there are a number of alternatives to creamed butter or margarine for raising a cake, all of which this volume has explored. One is a combination of eggs and sugar whisked over heat to incorporate air: *genoise,* the low-fat sponge leavened in this manner, is the foundation of many assembled creations. The *genoise* mixture does contain some saturated fat from egg yolks, but very much less than a sponge based on creamed butter. The *genoise* mixture is also high in cholesterol, but dietary cholesterol is probably of less concern nutritionally than saturated fat, which raises blood cholesterol indirectly: four medium-sized eggs provide less than a gram of cholesterol, whereas the same weight of butter provides 98 g of saturated fat.

Another alternative to using creamed butter for leavening is to rely on yeast, a microscopic organism that produces carbon dioxide gas as a by-product of its metabolism. A third ploy is to use a chemical leavener such as bicarbonate of soda or baking powder.

Because they lack large quantities of fat, the cakes would be dry were precautions not taken. But the recipes solve the problem of dryness with many alternative moistening agents.

Novel sweeteners

While limiting fat is the prime strategy for controlling the calorie count, limiting sugar is also a help. Of course a cake needs sweetness—that is part of its beguilement—but everyone can adjust to a shade less. This volume trains the palate gently in new ways, in some recipes by cutting down a little on quantities of sugar, elsewhere by offering replacements for the white sugar traditionally poured into cakes. Sometimes the replacements provide extra flavour, sometimes fewer calories, and sometimes valuable nutrients in addition to calories.

Many of the recipes use brown instead of white sugar; brown sugar—whether dark or light, demerara crystals or sticky muscovado—has all the calories of white sugar, and negligible other nutrients, but its distinctive flavour makes a positive contribution to a cake and renders sweetness less important. One warning, however: brown sugar, because of its moisture content, is often lumpy and needs sifting before mixing with other ingredients. Black treacle and molasses, by-products of sugarrefining, have less sweetness but even more flavour and also a notable nutritional value: 10 g of black treacle or molasses—a reasonable helping incorporated into a slice of cake—contain 15 per cent of a person's daily iron requirements and 5 per cent of his or her calcium needs.

Many recipes in this volume use honey alongside or instead of sugar, and a few recipes rely entirely on dried fruits for sweetness. Fructose, the sugar in fruit and honey, has, weight for weight, the same number of calories as cane or beet sugar, but one and a half times the sweetening power. Recipes that depend on honey, fruit or powdered fructose for sweetness can thus contribute fewer calories while achieving the same sweetness. Dried fruits provide iron and fibre in addition to their sweetness.

The value of flour

Flour contributes a varying proportion—up to 50 per cent in some recipes—of the calories in these cakes. Nutritionists consider flour a far better source of calories than sugar, because flour consists mainly of complex carbohydrates—chains of simple sugars which are digested more slowly than pure sugar to satisfy hunger and provide energy for longer. Moreover, flour offers additional nutrients: about 10 per cent of wheat flour is protein, and flour is also rich in iron and the B vitamins. White flour—milled from the inner layers of the wheat grain—contains a small amount of bran, which provides dietary fibre wholemeal flour, milled from the entire grain, contains more than. double the amount of bran. Brown flour contains some of the grain's outer layer and is intermediate in fibre content between white and wholemeal flours. In this volume, plain flour is the term used for unbleached white flour.

Recipes for cakes leavened with yeast often—though not always—specify strong flour, whether plain or wholemeal; the high proportion of protein in strong flour forms a sturdy lattice that traps the bubbles of carbon dioxide very effectively. The result is a well risen, open-textured cake.

Embellishing the exterior

Hundreds of the calories in traditional cakes come from the outside—in frostings, cream layers, butter icings. Cakes must look beautiful and festive, yet good looks need not mean dietary extravagance. This volume offers myriad ideas for decoration light in calories and fat. Instead of a thick, solid layer, icing appears as a random dribble or a lattice of piped lines. Cream is replaced with a low-fat soft cheese which provides a real nutritional benefit in the shape of protein and calcium. Hazelnut marzipan sometimes appears in place of the more fattening almond version. The jam specified for fillings is without added sugar; such jam is usually sweetened with concentrated apple juice. If you prefer, you can use reduced-sugar jam, which still offers a saving in the number of calories.

Fruit, with its glowing colours and luscious contours, provides an endless source of decorative possibilities at minimal calorific expense. Because fresh fruit does not keep well once washed and sliced, it is advisable when decorating with fruit to do so at the last possible minute.

Like all cake recipes, those in this book rely on meticulous measurement and careful timing. Substitutions are possible in cake recipes, but within limits that do not affect the consistency and rising capacity of the finished product. In many of the recipes alternatives are offered that do succeed.

Baking requires the cook to stay alert, since cooking times for cakes are affected by the temperature of the raw ingredients are the material of the tin. Cooking times can also vary widely from oven to oven. But if you have a fan-assisted oven, which circulates heat more quickly than a conventional oven, it is usually better to keep to the recommended cooking time and reduce the oven temperature by up to 40°C (75°F); follow the manufacturer's guidelines scrupulously.

Though a few cakes, particularly the breadlike ones, are at their most delicious served warm, thorough cooling is as crucial for success with most cakes as correctly judged cooking times. A cake cut before it has cooled completely to room temperature develops a hard crust on the cut surface; a fruit cake cut while still warm will not be thoroughly bonded and may disintegrate On a warm cake, icing will not set and a cream or cheese topping will melt. Cooling times range from a few minutes for small cakes and 30 minutes for a sponge sandwich to approximately; hours for a large plain cake and 4 hours for a heavy fruit cake.

The Key to Better Eating

Home Cooking addresses the concerns of today's weight-conscious, health-minded cooks with recipes that take into account guidelines set by nutritionists. The secret of eating well, of course, has to do with maintaining a balance of foods in the diet. The recipes thus should be used thoughtfully, in the context of a day's eating. To make the choice easier, an analysis is given of nutrients in a single serving. The counts for calories, protein, cholesterol, total fat, saturated fat and sodium are approximate.

Interpreting the chart

The chart below gives dietary guidelines for healthy men, women and children. Recommended figures vary from country to country, but the principles are the same everywhere. Here, the average daily amounts of calories and protein are from a report by the UK Department of Health and Social Security; the maximum advisable daily intake of fat is based on guidelines given by the National Advisory Committee on Nutrition Education (NACNE); those for cholesterol and sodium are based on upper limits suggested by the World Health Organization.

The volumes in the Home Cooking series do not purport to be diet books, nor do they focus on health foods. Rather, they express a common-sense approach to cooking that uses salt, sugar, cream, butter and oil in moderation while employing other ingredients that also provide flavour and satisfaction. The portions themselves are modest in size.

The recipes make few unusual demands. Naturally they call for fresh ingredients, offering substitutes when these are unavailable. (The substitute is not calculated in the nutrient analysis, however.)

Most of the ingredients can be found in any well-stocked supermarket.

Heavy-bottomed pots and pans are recommended to guard against burning whenever a small amount of oil is used and where there is danger of the food adhering to the hot surface, but non-stick pans can be utilized as well. Both safflower oil and virgin olive oil are favoured for sautéing. Safflower oil was chosen because it is the most highly polyunsaturated vegetable fat available in supermarkets, and polyunsaturated fats reduce blood cholesterol; if unobtainable, use sunflower oil, also high in polyunsaturated fats. Virgin olive oil is used because it has a fine fruity flavour lacking in the lesser grade known as "pure". In addition, it is—like all olive oil—high in mono-unsaturated fats, which are thought not to increase blood cholesterol. When virgin olive oil is unavailable, or when its flavour is not essential to the success of the dish, 'pure' may be used.

About cooking times

To help planning, time is taken into account in the recipes. While recognizing that everyone cooks at a different speed and that stoves and ovens differ, approximate "working" and "total" times are provided. Working time stands for the minutes actively spent on preparation; total time includes unattended cooking time, as well as time devoted to marinating, steeping or soaking ingredients. Since the recipes emphasize fresh foods, they may take a bit longer to prepare than 'quick and easy' dishes that call for canned or packaged products, but the difference in flavour, and often in nutrition, should compensate for the little extra time involved.

Recommended Dietary Guidelines

Average Daily Intake			Maximum Daily Intake			
	Calories	Protein *grams*	Cholesterol *milligrams*	Total fat *grams*	Saturated fat *grams*	Sodium *milligrams*
Females 7-8	1900	47	300	80	32	2000*
9-11	2050	51	300	77	35	2000
12-17	2150	53	300	81	36	2000
18-54	2150	54	300	81	36	2000
55-74	1900	47	300	72	32	2000
Males 7-8	1980	49	300	80	33	2000
9-11	2280	57	300	77	38	2000
12-14	2640	66	300	99	44	2000
15-17	2880	72	300	108	48	2000
18-34	2900	72	300	109	48	2000
35-64	2750	69	300	104	35	2000
65-74	2400	60	300	91	40	2000

* (or 5g salt)

Almond-Apricot Fingers

Serves 18

Working time: about 30 minutes

Total time: about 2 hours

Calories 150, Protein 3g, Cholesterol 25mg, Total fat 9g,
Saturated fat 2g, Sodium 100mg

---

125 g/4 oz	*wholemeal flour*
2 tsp	*baking powder*
125 g/4 oz	*polyunsaturated margarine*
90 g/3 oz	*light muscovado sugar*
2	*eggs*
175 g/6 oz	*dried apricots, chopped and soaked for 30 minutes in boiling water*
60 g/2 oz	*ground almonds*
1/2 tsp	*almond extract*
30 g/1 oz	*flaked almonds*

Preheat the oven to 190°C (375°F or Mark 5). Line the base of a 30 by 20 cm (12 by 8 inch) baking tin with greaseproof paper and grease the paper.

Sift the wholemeal flour with the baking powder, adding the bran left in the sieve. Cream the margarine and sugar together in a bowl until fluffy. Beat in the eggs one at a time, adding 1 tablespoon of the flour mixture with each egg.

Drain the apricots thoroughly, reserving 1 tablespoon of the soaking liquid. Stir the apricots into the batter and fold in the remaining flour mixture, together with the ground almonds, almond extract and reserved apricot soaking liquid. Turn the mixture into the baking tin. Spread it evenly to the edges and sprinkle the flaked almonds over the top.

Bake the cake for 30 to 35 minutes, until it springs back when pressed in the centre. Turn the cake out on to a wire rack, remove the lining paper, then reverse the cake on to another rack to cool. Cut the cake into fingers when it has cooled.

Angel Cake Casket with Mango Filling

Serves 8
Working time: about 30 minutes
Total time: about 5 hours
Calories 150, Protein 3g, Cholesterol 0mg, Total fat 1g,
Saturated fat 0g, Sodium 40mg

5	egg whites
1/8 tsp	salt
175 g/6 oz	caster sugar
1/2	lemon, finely grated rind only
1 tbsp	fresh lemon juice
30 g/1 oz	plain flour
30 g/1 oz	cornflour
	icing sugar to decorate

Mango filling

1	mango
90 g/3 oz	fromage frais
1 1/2 tsp	gelatine

Preheat the oven to 180°C (350°F or Mark 4). Lightly grease a 22 by 12 cm (9 by 5 inch) loaf tin. Line its base with greaseproof paper and grease the paper.

Whisk the egg whites with the salt until the whites stand in stiff peaks. Whisk in 125 g (4 oz) of the caster sugar, 1 tablespoon at a time, until the mixture is thick and glossy, then whisk in the lemon rind and juice. Mix the remaining caster sugar with the flours and whisk this in, 1 tablespoon at a time.

Transfer the mixture to the prepared tin and bake it for 35 to 40 minutes until the cake is risen and firm to the touch. Leave it to cool in the tin.

Meanwhile, make the filling. Peel the mango and cut all the flesh away from the stone. Purée the fruit in a food processor or blender: there should be about 20 cl (7 fl oz). Mix the purée with the *fromage frais*. Sprinkle the gelatine on to 2 tablespoons of hot water in a small bowl and stand the bowl in a pan of simmering water for about 10 minutes. When the gelatine has absorbed the water, add a little of the fruit mixture to it. Stir the gelatine-fruit mixture into the bulk of the puree.

Cut down into the cake 2 cm (3/4 inch) from the sides to within 2 cm (3/4 inch) of the base. Scoop out the centre of the cake with a spoon, to leave a casket with walls and base about 2 cm (3/4 inch) thick. Pour the mango purée into the casket. Cover the purée with some of the angel cake trimmings to give the cake its original depth. Cover the cake with plastic film and chill it for at least 2 hours to allow the purée to set.

Using a palette knife, loosen the edges of the cake and invert it on to a platter. Dust with the icing sugar.

EDITOR'S NOTE: The mango purée may be replaced with a purée of fresh apricots, peaches or gooseberries.

Apple and Date Cake

Serves 14
Working time: about 20 minutes
Total time: about 4 hours
Calories 240, Protein 5g, Cholesterol 50mg, Total fat 7g,
Saturated fat 1g, Sodium 100mg

300 g/10 oz	*wholemeal flour*
3 tsp	*baking powder*
2 tsp	*ground mixed spice*
1/2 tsp	*grated nutmeg*
125 g/4 oz	*dark brown sugar*
250 g/8 oz	*dried dates, chopped*
500 g/1 lb	*dessert apples, peeled and cored*
15 cl/1/4 pint	*medium-sweet cider*
3	*eggs*
8 cl/3 fl oz	*safflower oil*
2 tbsp	*clear honey*

Preheat the oven to 180°C (350°F or Mark 4). Grease a deep, 20 cm (8 inch) round cake tin. Line the base with greaseproof paper and grease the paper.

Sift the flour and baking powder into a bowl, adding the bran left in the sieve. Stir in the mixed spice, nutmeg, sugar and dates. Grate half the apples and add them to the dry ingredients with the cider, eggs and oil. With a wooden spoon, beat the ingredients together thoroughly and turn them into the prepared tin.

Slice the remaining apples thinly and overlap the slices in two circles on top of the cake; stand a few slices upright in the centre. Bake for 1 1/4 to 1 1/2 hours, until a skewer inserted in the centre comes out clean.

Turn the cake on to a wire rack and remove the lining paper. While the cake is still warm, boil the honey for 1 minute in a small saucepan. Brush the apples with the honey, then leave the cake to cool.

Apple Cake with Currants

Serves 16

Working time: about 25 minutes

Total time: about 5 hours

Calories 240, Protein 3g, Cholesterol 35mg, Total fat 7g,
Saturated fat 1g, Sodium 110mg

175 g/6 oz	*plain flour*
1/2 tsp	*bicarbonate of soda*
1 tsp	*ground mixed spice*
1/2 tsp	*ground cinnamon*
125 g/4 oz	*wholemeal flour*
125 g/4 oz	*polyunsaturated margarine*
125 g/4 oz	*light brown sugar*
2	*eggs*
1 tbsp	*fresh lemon juice*
175 g/6 oz	*currants*
125 g/4 oz	*sultanas*
60 g/2 oz	*mixed candied peel, chopped*
1	*lemon, grated rind only*
250 g/8 oz	*dessert apples, peeled, cored and coarsely grated*
2 tbsp	*caster sugar*

Preheat the oven to 180°C (350°F or Mark 4). Grease a 20 cm (8 inch) round cake tin and line it with non-stick parchment paper.

Sift the plain flour into a bowl, together with the bicarbonate of soda, mixed spice and cinnamon. Mix in the wholemeal flour. In another bowl, cream the margarine and brown sugar until very pale and fluffy. With a wooden spoon, beat in the eggs one at a time, following each with 1 tablespoon of the flour mixture, then add the lemon juice and fold in the remaining flour. Add the currants, sultanas, mixed candied peel, lemon rind and grated apples, and mix all the ingredients together thoroughly.

Spoon the mixture into the prepared tin and level the top. Sprinkle the caster sugar evenly over the surface of the cake. Cook the cake for 1 1/4 to 1 1/2 hours until golden-brown and firm to the touch. Leave the cake in the tin for 10 minutes, then turn it out on to a wire rack and leave until cool before removing the lining paper.

Apricot and Pine-Nut Roll

THIS CAKE IS FILLED AND ROLLED AS SOON AS IT COMES OUT OF THE
OVEN, WHILE THE SPONGE IS STILL FLEXIBLE, SO THE FILLING MUST BE
PREPARED BEFORE THE SPONGE IS COOKED.

Serves 12

Working time: about 40 minutes

Total time: about 1 hour and 15 minutes

Calories 145, Protein 5g, Cholesterol 35mg, Total fat 5g,
Saturated fat 0g, Sodium 50mg

---

175 g/6 oz	*dried apricots*
30 cl/¹/₂ pint	*fresh orange juice*
2 tbsp	*plain low-fat yoghurt*
2	*eggs*
60 g/2 oz	*light brown sugar*
60 g/2 oz	*brown flour*
¹/₂ tsp	*baking powder*
90 g/3 oz	*pine-nuts, finely ground*
2	*egg whites*
1 tbsp	*caster sugar*

Preheat the oven to 180°C (350°F or Mark 4). Grease a 32 by 22 cm (13 by 9 inch) Swiss roll tin. Line it with greaseproof paper and grease the paper.

Put the apricots and orange juice in a saucepan. Bring the juice to the boil and simmer the apricots for about 10 minutes, until they are tender and have absorbed nearly all the orange juice. Leave the fruit to cool for 10 minutes, then purée it with the yoghurt in a blender or food processor. Set aside.

Put the eggs and brown sugar in a bowl set over a pan of hot, but not boiling, water. Whisk by hand or with an electric mixer until the mixture is thick and creamy. Remove the bowl from the pan and continue to whisk until the whisk, when lifted, leaves a trail on the mixture's surface. Sift the flour with the baking powder into another bowl, and mix in 60 g (2 oz) of the pine-nuts. In a third bowl, whisk the egg whites until stiff, but not dry. Fold the flour mixture, together with one third of the whites, into the whisked eggs and sugar. Then fold in the remaining whites.

Pour the mixture into the prepared tin and tap the tin against the work surface to level the sponge. Bake the batter in the centre of the oven for 10 to 15 minutes, until well risen, lightly browned and springy when touched in the centre. Meanwhile, place a piece of greaseproof paper on the work surface. Mix the remaining pine-nuts with the caster sugar and sprinkle them evenly on the paper.

As soon as the cake comes out of the oven, invert it on to the nuts. Working quickly, detach the lining paper from the cake and trim away the crisp edges on all four sides. Spread the apricot purée to the edge of the long sides and to within 5 mm (¹/₂ inch) of the short sides. With the help of the paper, roll the cake

up, starting at one short side. Grip the roll for 30 seconds, until it holds its shape. Put the roll on a wire rack to cool.

EDITOR'S NOTE: Four large oranges will yield about 30 cl (10 fl oz) of orange juice.

14

Banana and Cardamom Cakes

Makes 18 cakes
Working time: about 20 minutes
Total time: about 50 minutes
Per cake: Calories 145, Protein 3g, Cholesterol 25mg,
Total fat 9g, Saturated fat 2g, Sodium 115mg

125 g/4 oz	*polyunsaturated margarine*
90 g/3 oz	*brown sugar*
10	*cardamom pods, seeds only, finely chopped*
125 g/4 oz	*wholemeal flour*
2 tsp	*baking powder*
2	*eggs*
2	*medium bananas, mashed*
60 g/2 oz	*ground almonds*

Creamy topping

90 g/3 oz	*medium-fat curd cheese*
2 tsp	*clear honey*
1 tbsp	*plain low-fat yoghurt*

Preheat the oven to 190°C (375°F or Mark 5). Grease and flour 18 bun tins.

In a bowl, cream the margarine and sugar together with the cardamom seeds until the mixture is fluffy. Sift the flour with the baking powder, adding the bran left in the sieve. With a wooden spoon, beat the eggs into the margarine and sugar one at a time, adding a tablespoon of the flour with each egg. Beat in the bananas and almonds, then fold in the remaining flour.

Divide the batter among the bun tins and bake the cakes for 15 minutes, until the centres spring back when pressed. Loosen the cakes from the tins with a small knife and put them on a wire rack to cool.

To make the topping, beat the curd cheese with the honey and yoghurt. When the blend is smooth, spoon it into a piping bag fitted with a medium-sized star nozzle and pipe a rosette on each cake.

15

Banana Layer Cake

Serves 12
Working time: about 30 minutes
Total time: about 2 hours
Calories 235, Protein 5g, Cholesterol 45mg, Total fat 11g,
Saturated fat 2g, Sodium 70mg

90 g/3 oz *soft brown sugar*
10 cl/3^1/$_2$ fl oz *safflower oil*
2 *eggs*
3 *bananas, peeled and mashed*
1 tsp *finely grated lemon rind*
175 g/6 oz *wholemeal flour*
1^1/$_2$ tsp *baking powder*
^{1}/$_4$ tsp *ground allspice*
60 g/2 oz *rolled oats*
^{1}/$_2$ tsp *icing sugar*

Yoghurt-banana filling

175 g/6 oz *thick Greek yoghurt*
1 *banana, peeled and finely chopped*

Preheat the oven to 180°C (350°F or Mark 4). Grease a 22 by 18 cm (9 by 7 inch) cake tin; line the base with greaseproof paper and grease the paper.

Whisk together the brown sugar, oil and eggs until thick and pale. Stir in the mashed bananas and lemon rind. Sift the flour with the baking powder and allspice into the banana mixture, adding the bran left in the sieve. Add the oats and then fold the ingredients together with a metal spoon. Transfer the batter to the prepared tin and level the surface. Bake the banana cake for about 30 minutes, until risen and firm to the touch. Leave it in the tin for 10 minutes, then transfer it to a wire tray to cool.

Remove the paper and trim the edges. Split the cake in half horizontally and halve each piece again.

To make the filling, mix the yoghurt with the chopped banana. Sandwich the four layers of cake together with the banana mixture and dust the top of the cake with the icing sugar.

Banana Tofu Cake

TOFU, ALSO KNOWN AS BEAN CURD, IS A PROTEIN-RICH EXTRACT OF SOYA BEANS. IT HAS A MILD TASTE AND A TEXTURE SIMILAR TO THAT OF CURD CHEESE. AGAR, A SEAWEED PRODUCT, HAS GELLING PROPERTIES AND IS USED BY VEGETARIANS IN PLACE OF GELATINE.

Serves 10
Working time: about 30 minutes
Total time: about 3 hours
Calories 290, Protein 20g, Cholesterol 20mg, Total fat 10g, Saturated fat 4g, Sodium 35mg

175 g/6 oz	*stoned fresh dates, chopped*
30 cl/$^1/_2$ pint	*fresh orange juice*
175 g/6 oz	*peeled bananas, sliced*
500 g/1 lb	*tofu*
1 tbsp	*agar flakes*
1 tsp	*finely grated lemon rind*
$^1/_2$ tsp	*ground mixed spice*
1 tbsp	*apricot jam without added sugar*
1 tbsp	*finely chopped skinned toasted hazelnuts*
Spicy oat base	
125 g/4 oz	*wholemeal flour*
125 g/4 oz	*rolled oats*
75 g/2$^1/_2$ oz	*unsalted butter, melted*
30 g/1 oz	*malt extract*
1 tsp	*ground mixed spice*

Preheat the oven to 180°C (350°F or Mark 4). To make the spicy oat base, combine the flour, oats, butter, malt extract and mixed spice in a bowl. Press them into the bottom of a 20 cm (8 inch) springform tin. Bake the base for 15 minutes, then leave it to cool.

Simmer the dates in the orange juice for about 12 minutes, until the dates are very soft. Put the dates and juice in a food processor or blender together with the bananas, tofu, agar flakes, lemon rind and mixed spice. Blend to a purée. Spoon the purée over the oat base and level the surface. Bake the cake for 40 to 45 minutes, until it is firm when pressed in the centre. Leave the cake to cool in the tin.

While the cake is cooling, heat the apricot jam in a small saucepan. Sieve the jam into a bowl and brush it over the surface of the cake. Sprinkle the chopped hazelnuts round the edge of the cake.

EDITOR'S NOTE: Two large peeled bananas weigh about 175 g (6 oz). Four large oranges yield about 30 cl ($^1/_2$ pint) of juice. To toast and skin hazelnuts, place them on a baking sheet in a 180°C (350°F or Mark 4) oven for 10 minutes. Enfold the nuts in a towel and loosen the skins by rubbing briskly.

Banana Walnut Cake

Serves 14

Working time: about 40 minutes

Total time: about 4 hours

Calories 285, Protein 4g, Cholesterol 25mg, Total fat 15g,
Saturated fat 3g, Sodium 125mg

125 g/4 oz	plain flour
4 tsp	baking powder
125 g/4 oz	wholemeal flour
150 g/5 oz	light brown sugar
75 g/2½ oz	shelled walnuts
125 g/4 oz	carrots, finely grated
175 g/6 oz	peeled bananas, mashed
1	egg
8 cl/3 fl oz	safflower oil

Lemon butter icing

45 g/1½ oz	unsalted butter
45 g/1½ oz	medium-fat curd cheese
¼ tsp	grated lemon rind
90 g/3 oz	icing sugar

Preheat the oven to 180°C (350°F or Mark 4). Line an 18 cm (7 inch) square cake tin with non-stick parchment paper.

Sift the plain flour and baking powder into a bowl and mix in the wholemeal flour and brown sugar. Finely chop 45 g (1½ oz) of the walnuts and stir them in, together with the carrots. Using a wooden spoon, beat the mashed bananas with the egg and oil in a separate bowl. Make a well in the centre of the dry ingredients, add the banana mixture and beat the batter until it is evenly blended.

Turn the batter into the tin, level the top and cook the cake for about 1 hour, until it is well browned and firm to the touch; a skewer inserted in the centre should come out clean. Turn the cake out on to a wire rack and leave it to cool with the paper still attached.

To make the lemon butter icing, beat the butter with a wooden spoon until soft, then beat in the curd cheese and lemon rind. Sift in enough icing sugar to give a spreading consistency. Remove the paper from the cake and turn the cake the right way up. Spread the icing over the top of the cake, swirling it with a round-bladed knife. Break the remaining walnuts into large pieces and sprinkle them over the icing.

EDITOR'S NOTE: Two bananas weigh approximately 175 g (6 oz) when peeled.

Caraway Seed Sponge

Serves 12
Working time: about 25 minutes
Total time: about 3 hours and 30 minutes
Calories 125, Protein 3g, Cholesterol 60mg, Total fat 3g,
Saturated fat 0g, Sodium 70mg

3	eggs, separated
150 g/5 oz	light brown sugar
125 g/4 oz	plain flour
1 tsp	baking powder
1½ tbsp	cornflour
2 tsp	polyunsaturated margarine
1 tbsp	orange flower water
1 tsp	caraway seeds
	icing sugar to decorate

Preheat the oven to 200°C (400°F or Mark 6). Grease a 20 cm (8 inch) round cake tin or a petal cake tin approximately 18 cm (7 inches) in diameter. Line the tin with non-stick parchment paper.

Whisk the egg whites until they stand in firm peaks. Gradually whisk in the brown sugar, 1 tablespoon at a time, then quickly fold in the egg yolks. Sift the flour, baking powder and cornflour together two or three times into another bowl, to aerate them very thoroughly. Heat the margarine in a small saucepan until the margarine melts, then remove the pan from the heat and add the orange flower water and 2 tablespoons of water. Using a metal spoon or a rubber spatula, fold the flour mixture quickly and evenly into the cake mixture, followed by the melted mixture and the caraway seeds. Pour the batter into the prepared tin and bake, until well risen, golden brown and firm to the touch—25 to 30 minutes in the round tin, or 30 to 40 minutes in the petal tin.

Turn the cake out on to a wire rack and leave it to cool, then remove the paper. Before serving the cake, sift icing sugar lightly over the top.

Candied Fruit Cake Squares

Makes 64 squares
Working time: about 1 hour
Total time about 5 hours and 30 minutes (includes drying)
Per square: Calories 50, Protein trace, Cholesterol 10mg,
Total fat 1g, Saturated fat trace, Sodium 15mg

1	*large thick-skinned grapefruit, peel only*
175 g/6 oz	*light brown sugar*
125 g/4 oz	*stoned dates, cut into 1 cm (¹/₂ inch)* *pieces*
100 g/3¹/₂ oz	*red glacé cherries, halved*
60 g/2 oz	*candied green figs or angelica, cut into* *strips*
100 g/3¹/₂ oz	*shelled walnuts, roughly chopped*
125 g/4 oz	*raisins*
3	*eggs, beaten*
125 g/4 oz	*muscovado sugar*
1 tsp	*pure vanilla extract*
1	*lemon, grated rind only*
100 g/3¹/₂ oz	*plain flour*
1 tsp	*baking powder*
1 tsp	*ground cinnamon*
¹/₂ tsp	*ground mixed spice*
3 tbsp	*brandy or whisky*
175 g/6 oz	*apricot jam*

Place the grapefruit peel in a saucepan, cover with cold water and bring slowly to the boil, then drain thoroughly. Repeat this process three more times to rid the peel of excess bitterness. Cover the peel with cold water once more, bring to the boil and simmer gently until the peel is soft but not breaking up—20 to 30 minutes. Drain the peel, reserving the water.

Prepare a syrup in a saucepan by dissolving the light brown sugar in 12.5 cl (4 fl oz) of the reserved water over a gentle heat. Add the peel and cook it gently, uncovered, for another 20 to 30 minutes, until it is completely translucent. Remove the peel from the pan and leave it on a wire rack for a few hours, until it is dry to the touch and easy to handle (or dry it for an hour in the oven at its lowest setting).

Preheat the oven to 170°C (325°F or Mark 3). Cut the dried peel into 1 cm (¹/₂ inch) pieces and place them in a large mixing bowl. Mix in the dates, cherries, figs, walnuts and raisins. In another bowl, blend the beaten eggs with the muscovado sugar, vanilla and lemon rind. Sift the flour with the baking powder, cinnamon and mixed spice into the bowl with the beaten eggs, and blend to a batter. Pour this mixture on to the fruit and stir well, ensuring that each piece of fruit is lightly covered with batter.

Line a shallow 25 cm (10 inch) square baking tin with non-stick parchment paper. Pour the mixture into the lined tin, level the surface and bake in the oven for about 1 hour, or until set. Remove the cake from the oven, prick the surface all over with a fork and dribble on the brandy. Leave to cool in the tin for 15 minutes before transferring to a wire rack to cool completely.

Cut the cake into 3 cm (1¹/₄ inch) squares. Heat the jam gently until it is liquid, then press it through a nylon sieve. Brush the glaze over and around each square.

EDITOR'S NOTE: Closely wrapped in foil, the cake may be left to mature for two days before it is cut into squares—this will give a moister result. If you are serving the cake without forks, brush the tops of the squares only with just 60 g (2 oz) of glaze to make them less sticky to handle. The squares will keep for about four weeks in an airtight container.

Carrot and Walnut Cake

THE FRUCTOSE IN THIS RECIPE POSSESSES ONE AND A HALF TIMES THE
SWEETENING POWER AS THE SAME WEIGHT OF SUGAR, BUT
CONTRIBUTES THE SAME NUMBER OF CALORIES.

Serves 8

Working time: about 30 minutes

Total time: about 2 hours

Calories 230, Protein 2g, Cholesterol 65mg, Total fat 12g,
Saturated fat 2g, Sodium 225mg

175 g/6 oz	*carrots, finely grated*
8 cl/3 fl oz	*safflower oil*
2 tbsp	*skimmed milk*
2	*eggs, beaten*
90 g/3 oz	*fructose*
90 g/3 oz	*plain flour*
1 tsp	*baking powder*
1 tsp	*bicarbonate of soda*
2 tsp	*ground cinnamon*
90 g/3 oz	*raisins*
15 g/¹/₂ oz	*shelled walnuts, chopped*
	icing sugar (optional)

Grease an 18 cm (7 inch) round cake dish and line it with greaseproof paper.

In a large bowl, mix the carrots well with the oil, skimmed milk, eggs and fructose. Sift in the flour together with the baking powder, bicarbonate of soda and cinnamon. Fold the dry mixture into the egg mixture, and blend in the raisins and walnuts. Spoon the batter into the cake dish.

Place the cake dish on an inverted saucer in the microwave. Cook the carrot cake on medium for 9 minutes, giving the dish a quarter turn every 3 minutes. Increase the power to high and microwave the cake for 2 to 3 minutes more, giving the dish a quarter turn after 1¹/₂ minutes. The cake is cooked when it shrinks from the sides of the dish. Leave the cake to stand for 10 minutes before turning it out of the dish to cool on a wire rack.

If you wish to decorate the cake, rest a wire rack on top of it and sift a little icing sugar over the cake from a sieve. Lift off the rack to reveal a stencil pattern.

Chiffon Cake with Raspberry-Cream Filling

CHIFFON SPONGE OBTAINS A THREEFOLD LEAVENING FROM BEATEN EGG WHITES, BAKING POWDER AND THE STEAM ESCAPING FROM A MOIST BATTER. OIL IS TRADITIONALLY USED IN THE MIXTURE; THIS RECIPE KEEPS THE PROPORTION VERY LOW.

Serves 16

Working time: about 35 minutes

Total time: about 1 hour and 20 minutes

Calories 210, Protein 3g, Cholesterol 45mg, Total fat 9g, Saturated fat 2g, Sodium 110mg

175 g/6 oz	*plain flour*
3 tsp	*baking powder*
125 g/4 oz	*caster sugar, plus 1 tbsp*
3 tbsp	*safflower oil*
3	*egg yolks*
6	*egg whites*

Fruit and cream filling

75 g/2¹/₂ oz	*caster sugar*
4	*fresh peaches, sliced*
2 tbsp	*brandy*
¹/₄ litre/8 fl oz	*whipping cream*
125 g/4 oz	*fresh raspberries*

Preheat the oven to 170°C (325°F or Mark 3). Grease two 20 cm (8 inch) round sandwich tins. Line the bases with greaseproof paper and grease the paper.

Sift the flour and baking powder into a bowl and mix in 125 g (4 oz) of the sugar. Make a well in the centre. In another bowl, whisk the oil and egg yolks with 5 tablespoons of water until well blended. Pour the egg yolk mixture into the dry ingredients and beat with a wooden spoon to create a smooth, glossy batter.

Whisk the egg whites until they are stiff but not dry. Add one third of the egg whites to the batter and fold them in using a spatula or large metal or plastic spoon. Then carefully fold in the remaining whites.

Divide the mixture equally between the two tins, and tap the tins to level the mixture. Bake the sponges in the centre of the oven, until well risen, lightly browned and springy when touched in the centre—about 20 minutes. Loosen the edges of the sponges with a palette knife, turn them out on to a wire rack and remove the paper. Leave until completely cool.

Meanwhile, prepare the filling. Put 60 g (2 oz) of the sugar and 15 cl (¹/₄ pint) of water in a wide, shallow saucepan. Heat gently, stirring, until the sugar dissolves, then bring the water to the boil. Boil the syrup gently for 4 to 5 minutes to reduce it slightly. Simmer the peach slices in the syrup for 1 to 2 minutes, until they begin to soften. Using a slotted spoon, transfer

the slices to kitchen paper to drain. Peel the slices. Stir 1 tablespoon of the brandy into the poaching syrup. Whisk the cream with the remaining sugar and brandy in a large bowl until the cream will hold soft peaks.

Set one of the sponge layers on a serving plate. Spoon half the syrup evenly over the sponge, then spread the sponge with half the whipped cream. Arrange the peach slices and raspberries on the cream. Spread the remaining cream over the fruit.

Leaving the remaining sponge upside down on the rack, spoon the remaining brandy syrup over it. Then turn it over and set it on the first layer. Sift the tablespoon of caster sugar over the cake.

EDITOR'S NOTE: To make a chocolate chiffon cake, replace 30 g (1 oz) of the flour with cocoa powder.

Chocolate Marble Cake

This is a variation on the traditional Madeira cake: a plain, dryish mixture that relies on butter for flavour. Here, to keep the saturated fat level down, a combination of butter and polyunsaturated margarine is used. The wrinkled surface of the marble cake is typical of all Madeira cakes and results from the dryness of the mixture.

Serves 20

Working time: about 20 minutes

Total time: about 3 hours

Calories 215, Protein 3g, Cholesterol 60mg, Total fat 13g, Saturated fat 5g, Sodium 145mg

350 g/12 oz	*plain flour*
3 tsp	*baking powder*
175 g/6 oz	*caster sugar*
150 g/5 oz	*unsalted butter*
125 g/4 oz	*polyunsaturated margarine*
4	*eggs*
1¹/₂ tbsp	*cocoa powder*

Preheat the oven to 170°C (325°F or Mark 3). Grease a 20 cm (8 inch) round cake tin. Line the tin with greaseproof paper and grease the paper.

Sift the flour and baking powder into a mixing bowl. Add the sugar, butter, margarine and eggs. Mix them together, then beat the batter with a wooden spoon for 2 to 3 minutes until it is smooth and glossy. Transfer half of the batter to another bowl.

Dissolve the cocoa in 3 tablespoons of boiling water and blend the paste until it is smooth. Add the cocoa mixture to one of the bowls of batter and stir to incorporate it. Then transfer alternate spoonfuls of plain and chocolate batter to the prepared cake tin. Tap the tin to level the batter and swirl a skewer through it to create a marbled effect.

Bake the cake in the centre of the oven, until risen, lightly browned and springy when touched in the centre—50 to 55 minutes. Loosen the edges with a small palette knife, turn the cake out of the tin on to a wire rack and remove the lining paper. Leave the cake to cool completely.

EDITOR'S NOTE: To vary the chocolate marble cake, add 1 teaspoon of grated orange rind to the plain batter. To make a coffee marble cake, replace the dissolved cocoa with 3 tablespoons of very strong black coffee.

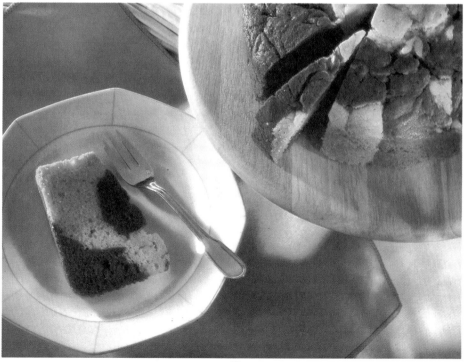

Cherry and Almond Sponge

Serves 16

Working time: about 25 minutes

Total time: about 26 hours

Calories 220, Protein 3g, Cholesterol 30g, Total fat 14g,
Saturated fat 3g, Sodium 115mg

175 g/6 oz	polyunsaturated margarine
175 g/6 oz	caster sugar
200 g/7 oz	plain flour
1¼ tsp	baking powder
30 g/1 oz	cornflour
30 g/1 oz	ground almonds
2	eggs
1 tbsp	lemon juice
45 g/1½ oz	flaked almonds
90 g/3 oz	glacé cherries, sliced

Preheat the oven to 170°C (325°F or Mark 3). Line an 18 cm (7 inch) square cake tin with non-stick parchment paper.

With a wooden spoon, cream the margarine and sugar together until very pale and fluffy. Sift the flour, baking powder and cornflour together into another bowl, then mix in the ground almonds. Beat the eggs into the creamed mixture, one at a time, following each with 1 tablespoon of the dry ingredients. Add the lemon juice and the remaining dry ingredients. Chop 30 g (1 oz) of the flaked almonds and stir them into the mixture, together with 60 g (2 oz) of the sliced cherries.

Turn the mixture into the prepared tin and level the top. Sprinkle the remaining flaked almonds and sliced cherries over the surface of the cake and cook it for 1¼ to 1½ hours, until firm to the touch and a light golden-brown. Test the cake with a skewer; if the skewer comes out clean, the cake is done. Leave the cake in the tin for a minute or two; it will shrink away from the sides. Turn the cake out on to a wire rack to cool. With the lining paper still in place, wrap the cake in foil and leave it for 24 hours before cutting it.

Spiced Sherry Cake

Serves 16

Working time: about 40 minutes

Total time: about 2 hours

Calories 180, Protein 3g, Cholesterol 15mg, Total fat 8g,
Saturated fat 2g, Sodium 115mg

175 g/6 oz	sultanas
4 tbsp	sherry
125 g/4 oz	polyunsaturated margarine
125 g/4 oz	light brown sugar
1	egg, beaten
175 g/6 oz	plain flour
1 tsp	bicarbonate of soda
½ tsp	ground cinnamon
½ tsp	grated nutmeg
⅛ tsp	ground cloves
45 g/1½ oz	shelled walnuts, finely chopped
125 g/4 oz	quark
2 tbsp	icing sugar
16	walnut halves

Preheat the oven to 180°C (350°F or Mark 4). Thoroughly grease two 20 cm (8 inch) round sandwich tins. Line their bases with greaseproof paper and grease the paper.

Put the sultanas in a saucepan with the sherry and 4 tablespoons of water and bring the liquid to the boil. Simmer the sultanas gently for about 5 minutes, until the liquid has been absorbed. Remove the pan from the heat and leave the sultanas to become cold, when they will release some of their liquid.

In a mixing bowl, cream the margarine and sugar until pale and fluffy, then beat in the egg with a wooden spoon. Sift the flour, together with the bicarbonate of soda, cinnamon, nutmeg and cloves, into another bowl. Gradually fold the spiced flour, alternately with the sultanas and their liquor, into the creamed margarine. Then fold in the chopped walnuts.

Divide the mixture between the prepared tins and level the surfaces. Cook the sponges for 30 to 35 minutes until firm to the touch. Leave them in the tins for 5 minutes, then loosen the edges of the sponges with a palette knife and turn them out on to a wire rack. Take care not to damage the sponges; the high proportion of liquid makes them very fragile. Leave the sponges to cool with the lining paper still attached.

Carefully peel off the paper and stand one sponge on a serving plate. Spread it with the quark and cover it with the second sponge layer. Dredge the top with the icing sugar and, with a sharp knife, mark the cake into 16 slices. Arrange the walnut halves in a circle round the top of the cake.

Cinnamon Rock Cakes

Most rock cake recipes call for about half as much fat as flour; this recipe cuts down on the butter, and substitutes yoghurt and skimmed milk for moisture. Because of their low fat content, these cakes do not keep well and should be eaten the day they are baked.

Makes 16 cakes
Working time: about 20 minutes
Total time: about 1 hour

Per cake: Calories 135, Protein 3g, Cholesterol 25mg, Total fat 4g, Saturated fat 2g, Sodium 90mg

125 g/4 oz	*plain flour*
2 tsp	*baking powder*
1/2 tsp	*grated nutmeg*
1 tsp	*ground cinnamon*
125 g/4 oz	*wholemeal flour*
60 g/2 oz	*dark brown sugar*
1	*lemon, finely grated rind only*
60 g/2 oz	*unsalted butter*
90 g/3 oz	*raisins*
90 g/3 oz	*sultanas*
1	*egg, beaten*
2 tbsp	*plain low-fat yoghurt*
6 tbsp	*skimmed milk*
2 tsp	*caster sugar*

Preheat the oven to 220°C (425°F or Mark 7). Butter and lightly flour two baking sheets.

Sift the plain flour, baking powder, nutmeg and half of the cinnamon into a bowl. Mix in the wholemeal flour, brown sugar and lemon rind. Rub the butter into the flours until the mixture resembles fine breadcrumbs. Mix in the raisins and sultanas, then make a well into the centre. Put the egg, yoghurt and milk into the well and stir to form a fairly soft mixture.

Space heaped teaspoons of the mixture well apart on the prepared baking sheets. Bake for 15 to 20 minutes until the rock cakes are well risen, golden-brown and firm to the touch. Transfer the rock cakes from the baking trays to wire racks to cool.

Mix the caster sugar with the remaining cinnamon and sprinkle the combination over the rock cakes.

Chocolate and Ginger Cheesecakes

Makes 6 cheesecakes
Working time: about 30 minutes
Total time: about 3 hours (includes chilling)
Per cheesecake: Calories 210, Protein 10g, Cholesterol 10mg, Total fat 9g, Saturated fat 5g, Sodium 230mg

45 g/1½ oz	*digestive biscuits*
75 g/2½ oz	*plain chocolate*
2 tsp	*powdered gelatine*
2 tbsp	*clear honey*
30 g/1 oz	*crystallized ginger*
300 g/10 oz	*quark*
6 cl/2 fl oz	*single cream*
1 tsp	*icing sugar, to decorate*

Cut six circles of greaseproof paper to line the bases of six 12.5 cl (4 fl oz) ramekins, using a ramekin as a guide. Break the biscuits into pieces, and process them briefly in a food processor. Break 45 g (1½ oz) of the chocolate into a basin and microwave it on medium for 2½ to 3 minutes, until melted. Stir until smooth, then combine with the biscuit crumbs. Divide the mixture among the ramekins, lightly pressing it into the bases. Chill until firm—about 20 minutes.

Sprinkle the gelatine over 2 tablespoons of water in a bowl and leave it to soften for 2 minutes. Microwave on high for 30 seconds, to melt the gelatine. Stir in the honey and cool slightly.

Meanwhile, very finely chop the ginger in a food processor and combine it with the quark and cream. Mix together until smooth, then blend in the gelatine mixture thoroughly. Divide among the ramekins, cover with plastic film and chill for at least 2 hours, or preferably overnight, until set.

For the topping, break the remaining chocolate into a basin and microwave it on medium for 2 to 2½ minutes. Stir the chocolate until smooth, then, using a metal spatula, spread it out very thinly on a marble slab or an inverted baking sheet. Leave to cool for 3 to 4 minutes, until almost set. Push a pastry scraper under the chocolate to produce scrolls.

Just before serving, slip a knife round the sides of the ramekins. Carefully unmould each cheesecake into the palm of your hand—to remove the lining paper—then place it on a board. Cover the cheesecakes with chocolate scrolls. Using a metal spatula to cover half the top of each cheesecake, sift icing sugar over the other half.

Coffee Butterfly Cakes

Makes 12 cakes
Working time: about 35 minutes
Total time: about 1 hour and 30 minutes
Per cake: Calories 180, Protein 2g, Cholesterol 20mg,
Total fat 9g, Saturated fat 5g, Sodium 45mg

---

125 g/4 oz *unsalted butter*
60 g/2 oz *light brown sugar*
60 g/2 oz *clear honey*
2 tbsp *strong black coffee*
2 *egg whites, lightly beaten*
175 g/6 oz *plain flour*
1½ tsp *baking powder*
15 cl/¼ pint *rum-flavoured pastry cream*
1 tsp *icing sugar*

Preheat the oven to 180°C (350°F or Mark 4). Butter 12 deep, sloping-sided bun tins. Dust the tins lightly with a little flour.

Use a wooden spoon or electric mixer to beat the butter in a bowl with the brown sugar and honey until soft. Add the black coffee and 1 tablespoon of warm water, and continue beating until the mixture becomes very light and fluffy. Gradually beat in the egg whites. Sift the flour and baking powder together over the creamed mixture, then fold them in carefully with a metal spoon or rubber spatula.

Divide the mixture evenly among the prepared tins. Bake the cakes for 15 to 20 minutes, until well risen, springy to the touch and very slightly shrunk from the sides of the tins. Leave the cakes in the tins for 2 to 3 minutes, then transfer them to a wire rack to cool.

Using a small, sharp, pointed knife held at an angle, carefully cut a cone out of the centre of each cake. Cut each cone in half.

Put the rum-flavoured pastry cream in a piping bag fitted with a medium-sized star nozzle. Pipe a whirl of pastry cream into the middle of each cake. Then replace the two halves of each cone on top of the cream, angling them to mimic butterfly wings. Sift the icing sugar lightly over the cakes.

Coffee Walnut Cake

Serves 14

Working time: about 20 minutes

Total time: about 2 hours and 30 minutes

Calories 210, Protein 4g, Cholesterol 30mg, Total fat 13g, Saturated fat 2g, Sodium 185mg

---

125 g/4 oz	*polyunsaturated margarine*
60 g/2 oz	*light brown sugar*
4 tbsp	*clear honey*
2	*eggs, beaten*
2 tbsp	*strong black coffee, cooled*
250 g/8 oz	*brown flour*
3 tsp	*baking powder*
90 g/3 oz	*shelled walnuts, roughly chopped*
10	*shelled walnut halves*

Preheat the oven to 170°C (325°F or Mark 3). Grease a deep 20 cm (8 inch) round cake tin. Line it with greaseproof paper and grease the paper.

Put the margarine, sugar and honey into a mixing bowl. Beat them together with a wooden spoon until light and fluffy. Add the beaten egg a little at a time, beating well after each addition. Beat in the coffee.

Sift the brown flour and baking powder into the batter. Using a spatula or large metal spoon, fold the flour into the batter, then mix in the chopped walnuts. Spoon the cake mixture into the prepared tin. Level the top with a small palette knife and arrange the walnut halves round the edge.

Bake the cake in the centre of the oven until risen, lightly browned and springy when touched in the centre—50 to 55 minutes. Loosen the edges of the cake with a small palette knife, turn it out on to a wire rack and remove the greaseproof paper. Leave the cake to cool before serving.

Cool Caribbean Cake

Serves 10

Working time: about 40 minutes

Total time: about 5 hours

Calories 180, Protein 4g, Cholesterol 5mg, Total fat 5g,
Saturated fat 2g, Sodium 95mg

60 g/2 oz	*plain chocolate*
2 tsp	*clear honey*
15 g/¹/₂ oz	*unsalted butter*
125 g/4 oz	*breakfast wheat flakes*
2 tbsp	*whipped cream*
1 tbsp	*coconut flakes*

Coconut ice cream

60 g/2 oz	*creamed coconut*
2 tbsp	*clear honey*
15 cl/¹/₄ pint	*plain low-fat yoghurt*
1	*egg white*

Mango ice cream

2	*mangoes, peeled and chopped*
4 tbsp	*fresh orange juice*
2 tbsp	*clear honey*
15 cl/¹/₄ pint	*plain low-fat yoghurt*
1	*egg white*

Line an 18 cm (7 inch) round cake tin with non-stick parchment paper. Half-fill a small saucepan with water and bring it to the boil; remove it from the heat. Put the chocolate, honey and butter in a bowl over the saucepan of hot water. Stir occasionally until the chocolate and butter have melted. Add the wheat flakes and stir to coat them with the chocolate mixture. Spread the chocolate wheat flakes in the base of the prepared tin. Level the layer with the back of a spoon and press it well down. Put the tin in the freezer.

To make the coconut ice cream, put 15 cl (¹/₄ pint) of water in a small saucepan and bring it to the boil. Remove the water from the heat and stir in the creamed coconut and the honey. Leave the blend to cool completely, then stir in the yoghurt and pour the mixture into a shallow plastic container. Place the coconut ice cream in the freezer and leave it until firm but not frozen hard—about 1 hour.

Meanwhile, make the mango ice cream. Purée the mangoes with the orange juice, honey and yoghurt in a blender or food processor. Pour the purée into a shallow plastic container and place it in the freezer. Leave it until firm but not frozen hard—1 to 2 hours.

Remove the coconut ice cream from the freezer. To break down the crystals, put the ice cream in a bowl and whisk it until smooth, or blend it in a food processor. Whisk the egg white until stiff in a separate bowl, then whisk the egg white into the ice cream. Pour the ice cream over the chocolate wheat flakes and freeze the two layers until firm but not frozen hard.

When the coconut layer is almost set, remove the mango ice cream from the freezer. Put it in a bowl and whisk it until smooth, or blend it in a food processor. Whisk the egg white until stiff in a separate bowl, then whisk the egg white into the ice cream. Pour the mango ice cream on top of the frozen layers of coconut ice cream and chocolate flakes and return the cake to the freezer until frozen—about 2 hours.

About 40 minutes before serving the cake, dip the base of the tin in warm water for a second and turn the cake out. Peel off the parchment paper and turn the cake on to a plate. Spoon the whipped cream into a piping bag fitted with a small star nozzle. Pipe whirls of cream round the top edge of the cake and decorate the cake with the coconut flakes. Leave the cake in the refrigerator to soften for 30 minutes before serving it.

EDITOR'S NOTE: If precooked breakfast wheat flakes are not available, substitute raw wheat flakes. Before stirring them into the chocolate mixture, toast them for 2 to 3 minutes under a medium grill. Creamed coconut, available in many supermarkets, is prepared from the puréed flesh of the nut.

Courgette Cake

THE COURGETTES IN THIS CAKE SUPPLY MOISTURE AND A FLAVOUR THAT MARRIES REMARKABLY WELL WITH THE SWEET INGREDIENTS.

Serves 12

Working time: about 15 minutes

Total time: about 2 hours and 30 minutes

Calories 225, Protein 4g, Cholesterol 25mg, Total fat 9g, Saturated fat 3g, Sodium 155mg

250 g/8 oz	*courgettes, coarsely grated*
125 g/4 oz	*fresh dates, stoned and chopped*
60 g/2 oz	*raisins*
4 tbsp	*clear honey*
125 g/4 oz	*polyunsaturated margarine*
125 g/4 oz	*light brown sugar*
1	*egg, beaten*
250 g/8 oz	*brown flour*
2 tsp	*baking powder*

Preheat the oven to 170°C (325°F or Mark 3). Grease a shallow 22 cm (9 inch) cake tin. Line its base with greaseproof paper and grease the paper.

Stir the courgettes with the dates, raisins and honey in a mixing bowl. In another bowl, cream the margarine and sugar together until light and fluffy.

Add the eggs with 2 tablespoons of water, and beat with a wooden spoon until the mixture is smooth and glossy.

Sift the flour with the baking powder, and fold them into the creamed margarine mixture using a spatula or large spoon. Then fold in the courgettes, dates and raisins. Spoon the mixture into the prepared tin and level the top with a small palette knife. Bake the courgette cake in the centre of the oven until risen, lightly browned and springy when touched in the centre— 55 to 60 minutes.

Loosen the cake from the sides of the tin with a small palette knife. Turn the cake on to a wire rack and remove the lining paper. Leave the cake until it has cooled completely before serving.

Dundee Cake

WITH ITS VERY HIGH PROPORTION OF FRUIT, THIS MOIST, DARK CAKE IS FULL OF FLAVOUR YET LIGHT IN TEXTURE.

Working time: about 20 minutes

Total time: about 7 hours

Calories 215, Protein 3g, Cholesterol 40mg, Total fat 8g, Saturated fat 2g, Sodium 95mg

250 g/8 oz	currants
250 g/8 oz	sultanas
250 g/8 oz	raisins
60 g/2 oz	mixed candied peel, chopped
60 g/2 oz	glacé cherries, quartered
1	orange, grated rind and juice
250 g/8 oz	wholemeal flour
1 tsp	baking powder
90 g/3 oz	medium oatmeal
2 tsp	ground mixed spice
125 g/4 oz	light brown sugar
2 tbsp	molasses
175 g/6 oz	polyunsaturated margarine
4	eggs, beaten
60 g/2 oz	blanched almonds

Preheat the oven to 140°C (275°F or Mark 1) Grease a deep, 18 cm (7 inch) square cake tin and double-line it with greaseproof paper. Grease the paper. To prevent the sides and base of the cake from scorching during the long cooking, tie a double thickness of brown paper round the outside of the tin and stand the tin on a baking sheet double-lined with brown paper.

Stir the currants, sultanas, raisins, mixed peel, glacé cherries, orange rind and juice together in a mixing bowl. Sift the flour and baking powder together into another bowl, adding the bran left in the sieve. Mix in the oatmeal, mixed spice, sugar, molasses, margarine and eggs. Beat the mixture with a wooden spoon for 2 to 3 minutes until smooth and glossy.

Stir the fruit into the cake batter. Spoon the batter into the cake tin and level the top with a small palette knife. Arrange the almonds in rows on the cake.

Bake the cake in the centre of the oven until risen and dark brown—2$^1\!/_2$ to 3 hours. Test the cake by inserting a warm skewer or cocktail stick into the centre of the cake. If it is clean when removed, the cake is cooked; otherwise, return the cake to the oven and test it at 15-minute intervals.

Leave the cake to cool in the tin, then turn it out and remove the lining paper.

EDITOR'S NOTE: Because the fruit retains moisture, this cake will keep for up to one month if wrapped in plastic film or foil and stored in a cold, dry place.

Espresso Cakes

Makes 8 cakes

Working (and total) time: about 25 minutes

Per cake: Calories 225, Protein 7g, Cholesterol 120mg,
Total fat 8g, Saturated fat 4g, Sodium 55mg

1	*genoese sponge, 1 teaspoon of brandy added to uncooked batter*
2 tbsp	*brandy*
4 tbsp	*very strong black coffee (not instant coffee)*
15 cl/¹/₄ pint	*liqueur-flavoured pastry cream, flavoured with brandy*
15 g/¹/₂ oz	*cocoa powder*
15 g/¹/₂ oz	*coffee beans, finely ground*
8	*chocolate coffee-bean sweets*

Trim off the four outer crusts from the edge of the cooked sponge. Using a long, sharp knife, cut the sponge in half horizontally, making two large sheets. Combine the brandy and black coffee and, using a pastry brush, lightly paint the mixture on to the cut faces of the sponge sheets. Cut each sheet crosswise through the centre, making four rectangles in all.

Spread one third of the brandy flavoured pastry cream over the cut surface of one of the rectangles, bringing it right up to the edges. Arrange a second rectangle, cut side down, over the cream. Spread on another third of the filling. Lay the third rectangle, cut side up, over the cream. Smooth on the last of the filling, then set the final rectangle, cut side down, on the top. Using a long, sharp knife, halve the assembly lengthwise, then cut each half crosswise into four equal pieces, to give a total of eight cakes.

Place the espresso cakes in a straight line and cover half of each one with a sheet of paper or thin card. Sift the cocoa powder over the exposed half of each cake; the layer of cocoa powder should be fairly thick or the liquid in the sponge will soak through and produce dark patches. Carefully move the paper or card to cover the cocoa topping and sift the finely ground coffee beans over the halves now exposed. Finally, decorate each espresso cake with a chocolate coffee-bean sweet.

34

Fairy Cakes

Makes 12 cakes
Working time: about 30 minutes
Total time: 1 hour and 15 minutes
Per plain, cherry or sultana cake: Calories 195, Protein 2g, Cholesterol 25mg, Total fat 8g, Saturated fat 2g, Sodium 160mg
Per coconut cake: Calories 205, Protein 3g, Cholesterol 25mg, Total fat 12g, Saturated fat 5g, Sodium 155mg

125 g/4 oz	*polyunsaturated margarine*
60 g/2 oz	*caster sugar*
60 g/2 oz	*clear honey*
1 tsp	*pure vanilla extract*
2	*egg whites, lightly beaten*
175 g/6 oz	*plain flour*
1¹/₂ tsp	*baking powder*
15 g/¹/₂ oz	*glacée cherries, chopped*
15 g/¹/₂ oz	*desiccated coconut*
30 g/1 oz	*sultanas*
15 cl/¹/₄ pint	*pastry cream*
1	*hazelnut, thinly sliced*
	chocolate curls for garnish

Preheat the oven to 190°C (375°F or Mark 5). Grease and lightly flour 12 deep, sloping-sided bun tins.

Put the margarine, sugar and honey in a bowl. With a wooden spoon, beat them until they are soft and creamy. Beat in the vanilla extract with 3 tablespoons of warm water; continue beating until the mixture becomes very light and fluffy. Gradually beat in the egg whites. Sift the flour and baking powder over the creamed mixture, then fold them in carefully with a metal spoon or rubber spatula.

Half fill three of the bun tins with the plain mixture. Divide the remaining mixture equally into three. To one third add the cherries, reserving three pieces; to another third add the coconut, reserving 2 teaspoons; to the remaining third, add the sultanas. Spoon the mixtures into the bun tins. Bake for 10 to 15 minutes until the fairy cakes are well risen, golden-brown and springy to the touch. Leave them in the tins for 2 to 3 minutes, then transfer them to wire racks.

When the cakes have cooled, put the pastry cream into a piping bag fitted with a medium-sized star nozzle. Pipe a shell shape on top of each cake. Decorate the plain cakes with the hazelnut slices, the cherry cakes with the reserved cherry pieces, the coconut cakes with the reserved coconut, and the sultana cakes with the chocolate curls.

Farmhouse Fruit Cake

THE OVERNIGHT SOAKING OF THE INGREDIENTS IN TEA MAKES THIS CAKE
VERY MOIST.

Serves 10

Working time: about 20 minutes

Total time: about 1^1/$_2$ days

Calories 210, Protein 2g, Cholesterol 0mg, Total fat 7g,
Saturated fat 2g, Sodium 170mg

250 g/8 oz	*plain flour*
^{1}/$_2$ tsp	*allspice*
90 g/3 oz	*polyunsaturated margarine*
90 g/3 oz	*light brown sugar*
125 g/4 oz	*sultanas*
60 g/2 oz	*currants*
^{1}/$_2$	*lemon, grated rind only*
1 tsp	*bicarbonate of soda*
2 tbsp	*lemon juice*
^{1}/$_4$ litre	*cold tea*
1 tsp	*sugar crystals*

Grease a 16 to 18 cm (6^1/$_2$ to 7 inch) round cake tin and line it with non-stick parchment paper.

Sift the flour and allspice together in a bowl. Add the margarine and rub it in until the mixture resembles fine breadcrumbs. Stir in the brown sugar, sultanas, currants and lemon rind until they are evenly distributed. Whisk the bicarbonate of soda into the lemon juice and add this mixture, together with the cold tea, to the dry ingredients. When the ingredients are thoroughly combined, turn the mixture into the prepared tin, level the top and leave the mixture to stand overnight.

The following day, preheat the oven to 170°C (325°F or Mark 3). Sprinkle the cake mixture with the sugar crystals and cook it for about 1^1/$_2$ hours, until a skewer inserted in its centre comes out clean. Turn the cake out on to a wire rack and leave it to cool. With the lining paper still in place, wrap the cake in foil and store it for 24 hours; it crumbles if sliced sooner.

Fig Cake Encased in Shortcrust

Serves 10
Working time: about 45 minutes
Total time: about 3 hours and 30 minutes
Calories 230, Protein 5g, Cholesterol 50mg, Total fat 11g,
Saturated fat 5g, Sodium 120mg

125 g/4 oz *dried figs, chopped*
125 g/4 oz *dried pears, chopped*
60 g/2 oz *dried dates, chopped*
30 g/1 oz *unsalted butter, diced*
2 tbsp *Armagnac*
60 g/2 oz *shelled walnuts, chopped*
1 *egg, beaten*
30 g/1 oz *plain flour*
$^1/_2$ tsp *ground cinnamon*
$^1/_4$ tsp *ground cloves*
$^1/_8$ tsp *salt*
icing sugar to decorate
Pastry crust
125 g/4 oz *plain flour*
60 g/2 oz *unsalted butter*
beaten egg white to glaze

Put the figs, pears and dates in a saucepan with 6 tablespoons of water. Simmer gently until the fruits are soft and the water has been absorbed—7 to 8 minutes. Add the butter to the pan and stir the mixture until the butter has melted. Let the fruit-butter mixture cool, then beat in the Armagnac, walnuts, egg, flour, cinnamon, cloves and salt. Set aside.

Preheat the oven to 180°C (350°F or Mark 4).

To make the pastry, sift the flour into a bowl. Rub in the butter and mix in 4 teaspoons of iced water to make a firm dough. Roll out two thirds of the pastry on a lightly floured surface to make a rectangle large enough to cover the base and sides of a 20 by 10 cm (8 by 4 inch) loaf tin. Transfer the pastry to the tin and press it against the base and sides of the tin to cover them with an even thickness.

Spoon the filling into the tin and level the surface. Trim the pastry level with the top of the tin, then fold the pastry walls in over the filling. Add the trimmings to the reserved pastry and roll it out to make a rectangle to fit the top of the cake exactly. Trim the edges of the pastry lid, brush with egg white and lay it, brushed side down, on the filling. Press the edge well so that it sticks to the overlapping pastry walls. Using a fork, mark a criss-cross pattern and decorative border on the pastry lid. Brush the lid with egg white.

Bake the cake for 40 to 45 minutes, until the pastry is pale golden. Let the cake stand in the tin for 10 minutes, then transfer it to a wire rack and leave it to cool. Dust the fig cake with icing sugar before serving.

Frosted Orange Cake

Serves 14

Working time: about 25 minutes

Total time: about 3 hours and 30 minutes

Calories 214, Protein 3g, Cholesterol 30mg, Total fat 7g, Saturated fat 2g, Sodium 100mg

300 g/10 oz *plain flour*

2¹/₂ tsp *baking powder*

125 g/4 oz *polyunsaturated margarine*

90 g/3 oz *light brown sugar*

2 *oranges, grated rind only*

2 *eggs*

3 tbsp *fresh orange juice*

Orange glacé icing

125 g/4 oz *icing sugar*

3 tsp *fresh orange juice*

¹/₂ *orange, grated rind only*

Preheat the oven to 170°C (325°F or Mark 3). Line an 18 cm (7 inch) round cake tin with non-stick parchment paper.

Sift the flour and baking powder together into a bowl and rub in the margarine until the mixture re-sembles fine breadcrumbs. Stir in the sugar and orange rind. In another bowl, beat the eggs and fresh orange juice together and then mix them into the dry ingredients with a wooden spoon. Turn the batter into the prepared tin and level the top. Bake the cake for about 1 hour, until well risen and firm to the touch; a skewer inserted in the centre of the cake should come out clean. Turn the cake on to a wire rack, leave it until cool and then peel off the paper.

To make the icing, sift the icing sugar into a bowl and beat in just enough of the orange juice to give a thick coating consistency. Spread the icing over the top of the cake, allowing it to run down the sides in places. Sprinkle the icing with the grated orange rind and leave the cake until the icing has set.

Grapefruit Cake

Serves 12
Working time: about 30 minutes
Total time: about 3 hours
Calories 240, Protein 4g, Cholesterol 65mg, Total fat 8g,
Saturated fat 2g, Sodium 100mg

125 g/4 oz *sultanas*
125 g/4 oz *raisins*
125 g/4 oz *currants*
          1 *grapefruit, rind finely grated, flesh*
             segmented and chopped
10 cl/3^1/$_2$ fl oz *fresh grapefruit juice*
90 g/3 oz *polyunsaturated margarine*
90 g/3 oz *dark brown sugar*
          2 *large eggs, beaten*
175 g/6 oz *plain flour*
          1 tbsp *clear honey*

Grease the base of an 18 cm (7 inch) round cake dish and line it with greaseproof paper.

Put the sultanas, raisins, currants, grapefruit rind and juice in a bowl. Cover the fruit and microwave it on high for 3 minutes, stirring once. Remove the cover and leave the fruit to cool slightly.

Meanwhile, in another bowl, cream the margarine with the sugar and eggs until light and fluffy. Fold in the flour and the dried fruit mixture, blending well. Lastly, fold in the grapefruit flesh. Spoon the mixture into the cake dish and level the surface.

Cover the dish and place it on an inverted plate in the microwave. Cook the cake on high for 10 minutes, giving the dish a quarter turn every 3 minutes. Remove the cover, reduce the power to defrost and cook for a further 4 to 6 minutes—or until a skewer inserted into the centre of the cake comes out clean.

Leave the grapefruit cake to stand for 20 minutes before turning it out on to a wire rack to cool. While the cake is still warm, brush the top with the honey.

EDITOR'S NOTE: One grapefruit will yield about 10 cl (3^1/$_2$ fl oz) of juice.

Harvest Cake

Serves 28

Working time: about 40 minutes

Total time: about 7 hours

Calories 185, Protein 5g, Cholesterol 30mg, Total fat 6g, Saturated fat 2g, Sodium 120mg

250 g/8 oz	*cooking apples, peeled, cored and chopped*
250 g/8 oz	*pears, peeled, cored and chopped*
250 g/8 oz	*plums, stoned and chopped*
175 g/6 oz	*raisins*
17.5 cl/6 fl oz	*apple juice or grape juice*
350 g/12 oz	*malted wheat flour*
175 g/6 oz	*light brown sugar*
175 g/6 oz	*polyunsaturated margarine*
2 tsp	*ground mixed spice*
3	*eggs*
150 g/5 oz	*wholewheat flakes*

Cheese and fruit topping

1	*green-skinned dessert apple*
1	*pear*
1 tbsp	*lemon juice*
175 g/6 oz	*quark*
1 tbsp	*plain low-fat yoghurt*
1 tsp	*clear honey*

Grease a 25 by 20 cm (10 by 8 inch) oblong tin. Line it with greaseproof paper and grease the paper. Mix the chopped apples, pears and plums with the raisins and apple juice or grape juice in a bowl. Cover the bowl and leave for up to 1 hour, to plump the fruit. Meanwhile, preheat the oven to 170°C (325°F or Mark 3).

Put the flour, sugar, margarine, mixed spice and eggs in a mixing bowl. Stir them together with a wooden spoon and beat the mixture until it is smooth and glossy. Add the soaked fruit and the wheat flakes to the cake mixture a little at a time, stirring well after each addition. Spoon the mixture into the prepared tin and level the top with a small palette knife. Bake the cake in the centre of the oven until risen, lightly browned and springy when touched in the centre— 1½ hours to 1¾ hours.

Loosen the edges of the cake with a small palette knife, turn it out of the tin on to a wire rack and remove the lining paper. Leave the cake to cool completely.

To make the cheese and fruit topping, core and thinly slice the apple and pear. Sprinkle the slices with lemon juice to stop discolouration. Put the quark in a bowl with the yoghurt and honey and blend them together. Spread the cheese mixture over the top of the cake and arrange alternate pairs of apple and pear slices down the centre.

Iced Sponge Cakes

Makes 30 cakes
Working time: about 1 hour and 25 minutes
Total time: about 1 hour and 40 minutes
Per cake: Calories 95, Protein 1g, Cholesterol 25mg, Total fat 3g, Saturated fat 1g, Sodium 10mg

3	*eggs*
90 g/3 oz	*caster sugar*
90 g/3 oz	*plain flour*
2 tsp	*strong black coffee, cooled*
1/2 tsp	*pure almond extract*
1 tsp	*cocoa powder, sifted*
1 tbsp	*desiccated coconut*

Icings and toppings

100 g/3 1/2 oz	*plain chocolate, broken into pieces*
3	*crystallized violets, coarsely chopped*
15 g/1/2 oz	*hazelnuts, toasted and skinned, chopped*
250 g/8 oz	*icing sugar*
15 g/1/2 oz	*unsalted butter, melted*
1 tsp	*fresh lemon juice*
1/2	*orange, grated rind and 1 tsp juice only*
2 tsp	*strong black coffee, cooled*
15 g/1/2 oz	*flaked almonds, toasted*
1/2	*candied clementine, or other candied fruit, finely sliced*
15 g/1/2 oz	*plain chocolate scrolls*

Preheat the oven to 180°C (350°F or Mark 4). Lightly grease and flour 30 shallow tartlet tins of assorted shapes, each about 7.5 cm (3 inches) in diameter.

Place the eggs and caster sugar in a mixing bowl set over a pan of hot, but not boiling, water on a low heat. Using an electric hand-held mixer, whisk the eggs and sugar together until thick and pale. Remove the bowl from the heat and continue whisking until the mixture is cool and falls from the whisk in a ribbon trail. Sift the flour lightly over the surface of the mixture then fold it in gently.

Divide the mixture equally among five small bowls. Leave one portion plain and flavour each of the other by stirring in one of the four flavourings: coffee, almond extract, cocoa powder and desiccated coconut. Spoon the mixtures evenly into the prepared tins and bake until they are golden—10 to 15 minutes. Gently unmould them and leave to cool on a wire rack.

To ice the plain and coffee-flavoured cakes with chocolate icing, put the chocolate in a bowl with 6 tablespoons of water and place the bowl over a saucepan of simmering water until the chocolate melts, then stir. Let the chocolate cool and thicken slightly—about 5 minutes. Place one of the cakes on a metal spatula, hold it over the bowl and spoon the chocolate over it. Place the iced cake on a sheet of greaseproof paper. Ice the remaining plain and coffee-flavoured

cakes in the same way. Decorate each plain cake with a piece of crystallized violet and sprinkle chopped hazelnuts over the coffee-flavoured cakes, then leave the cakes to set.

To ice the remaining cakes, mix the icing sugar with the butter and 3 tablespoons of warm water. Divide this into three portions: flavour one with the lemon juice, one with the grated orange rind and orange juice, and the third with the coffee. Using the same technique as for the chocolate icing, cover the almond cakes with lemon icing, the coconut cakes with orange icing, and the chocolate cakes with coffee icing. Decorate them with the flaked almonds, candied clementines and chocolate scrolls respectively.

EDITOR'S NOTE: To toast flaked almonds, put them under the grill for about 2 minutes until golden, shaking them constantly.

Lemon Curd Cakes

Serves 12

Working time: about 45 minutes

Total time: about 1 hour and 45 minutes

Calories 170, Protein 2g, Cholesterol 60mg, Total fat 4g,
Saturated fat 2g, Sodium 25mg

3	*eggs*
1	*egg white*
125 g/4 oz	*caster sugar*
125 g/4 oz	*plain flour*
30 g/1 oz	*unsalted butter, melted and cooled*
3 tbsp	*lemon curd*

Piped frosting

250 g/8 oz	*caster sugar*
1	*egg white*

Preheat the oven to 180°C (350°F or Mark 4). Grease an oblong tin about 28 by 18 by 4 cm (11 by 7 by 1½ inches). Line the base with non-stick parchment paper.

Put the eggs, egg white and caster sugar in a large bowl. Place the bowl over a saucepan of hot, but not boiling, water on a low heat. Whisk the eggs and sugar by hand or with an electric mixer until thick and very pale. Remove the bowl from the heat and continue whisking until the mixture is cool and will hold a ribbon trail almost indefinitely. Sift the flour very lightly over the top of the whisked mixture and fold it in carefully with a large metal spoon or rubber spatula. Gradually fold in the melted butter.

Pour the sponge mixture into the prepared tin and spread it evenly. Bake the sponge for 25 to 30 minutes, until well risen, firm to the touch and very slightly shrunk away from the sides of the tin. Turn the sponge out on to a wire rack. Loosen but do not remove the parchment paper. Place another rack on top of the paper, then invert both the racks together so that the paper is underneath. Remove the top rack and leave the sponge to cool. Transfer the sponge on to a flat surface. Slice it in half horizontally and sandwich the two layers together with lemon curd.

To make the frosting, put the sugar in a saucepan with 7.5 cl (2½ fl oz) of cold water. Heat very gently until every granule of sugar has dissolved, brushing the sides of the pan down with hot water from time to time. Bring the syrup to the boil and cook it until its temperature reads 116°C (240°F) on a sugar thermometer. Meanwhile, whisk the egg white until it is very stiff but not dry. Immediately the sugar syrup reaches the required temperature, whisk the syrup into the egg white, pouring it in a steady stream from a height. Continue whisking until the frosting just loses its shine and becomes stiff enough to hold a peak.

Without delay, since the frosting begins to harden within a few minutes, spoon the frosting into a piping bag fitted with a seven-point 8 mm (5/16 inch) star nozzle. Pipe the frosting in diagonal lines across the cake. Pipe rows of stars between the lines. Slice the sponge into 12 when the frosting has set.

Madeleines

THIS RECIPE FOR THE SHELL-SHAPED SPONGE CAKES KNOWN AS
MADELEINES USES LESS EGG YOLK AND BUTTER THAN MORE
TRADITIONAL MIXTURES.

Makes 20 madeleines
Working time: about 10 minutes
Total time: about 35 minutes

Per madeleine: Calories 65, Protein 1g, Cholesterol 30mg,
Total fat 2g, Saturated fat 1g, Sodium 10mg

1	*egg*
1	*egg white*
90 g/3 oz	*caster sugar*
1 tbsp	*amaretto liqueur*
90 g/3 oz	*plain flour*
45 g/1½ oz	*unsalted butter, melted and cooled*
1 tbsp	*vanilla sugar*

Preheat the oven to 200°C (400°F or Mark 6). Butter twenty 7.5 cm (3 inch) madeleine moulds and dust them lightly with flour.

Put the egg and egg white into a bowl with the caster sugar and amaretto. Whisk the mixture until it thickens to the consistency of unwhipped double cream. Sift the flour lightly over the surface of the mixture, then fold it in very carefully with a metal spoon or rubber spatula. Gently fold in the melted butter.

Half fill each madeleine mould with mixture. Bake the madeleines for 15 to 20 minutes, until well risen, lightly browned and springy to the touch. Carefully turn them out of the moulds on to a wire rack and immediately sift the vanilla sugar over them. Serve the madeleines while still warm, or allow them to cool.

Orange and Lemon Ring Cake

THE FRUCTOSE IN THIS RECIPE POSSESSES ONE AND A HALF TIMES THE
SWEETENING POWER AS THE SAME WEIGHT OF SUGAR, BUT
CONTRIBUTES THE SAME NUMBER OF CALORIES.

Serves: 10

Working time: about 30 minutes

Total time: about 1 hour and 30 minutes

Calories 225, Protein 5g, Cholesterol 80mg, Total fat 11g,
Saturated fat 2g, Sodium 170mg

4	*digestive biscuits, crushed*
75 g/2¹/₂ oz	*fructose*
3	*eggs, beaten*
8 cl/3 fl oz	*safflower oil*
¹/₂	*lemon, grated rind only*
¹/₂	*small orange, grated rind only*
2 tbsp	*fresh lemon juice*
2 tbsp	*fresh orange juice*
175 g/6 oz	*plain flour*
2 tsp	*baking powder*

Orange garnish and glaze

1	*large orange, peel and all pith removed*
1 tbsp	*honey*

Lightly grease a 2 litre (3¹/₂ pint) fluted ring mould and coat it evenly with the biscuit crumbs. Put the fructose, eggs, oil, grated rind and juice into a bowl, sift in the flour and baking powder, and whisk them with an electric beater at low speed for about 30 seconds, until well blended and smooth.

Spoon the mixture into the prepared ring mould, taking care not to disturb the biscuit crumb coating. Microwave the cake on high for 4 to 5 minutes, giving the mould a quarter turn every minute, until the cake feels springy to the touch.

Leave the cake to stand for 10 minutes before turning it out on to a wire rack. While the cake cools, prepare the garnish. Slice the orange into segments, cutting on either side of the membrane; hold the orange over a bowl to catch the juice. To soften the segments, put them in a dish and microwave them on high for 1 to 1¹/₂ minutes. Add any juice that escapes from them to the juice already in the bowl.

To make the glaze, combine the honey with the juice from the orange and microwave the mixture on high for 30 seconds. When the cake is cool, brush it with the honey-orange glaze and decorate it with the orange segments.

Parsnip and Orange Cake

THE GRATED PARSNIP IN THIS RECIPE PROVIDES MOISTURE AND A HINT
OF CRUNCHINESS TO THE CAKE'S TEXTURE; THE DOMINANT FLAVOUR IS
ORANGE.

Serves 14
Working time: about 30 minutes
Total time: about 4 hours
Calories 210, Protein 5g, Cholesterol 40mg, Total fat 10g,
Saturated fat 2g, Sodium 240mg

125 g/4 oz	*polyunsaturated margarine*
125 g/4 oz	*brown sugar*
2 tbsp	*malt extract*
1	*orange, grated rind and juice only*
3	*eggs*
275 g/9 oz	*wholemeal flour*
1 tbsp	*baking powder*
250 g/8 oz	*parsnips, peeled and grated*
Orange topping	
90 g/3 oz	*medium-fat curd cheese*
2 tsp	*clear honey*
1	*orange, rind only, half grated, half julienned and blanched*

Preheat the oven to 170°C (325°F or Mark 3). Grease
a deep 20 cm (8 inch) round cake tin. Line the base
with greaseproof paper and grease the paper.

Cream the margarine, sugar, malt extract and orange rind until fluffy. Beat in the eggs one at a time,
adding 1 tablespoon of flour with each egg. Sift the
remaining flour with the baking powder, adding the
bran left in the sieve. Fold the flour, parsnips and orange juice into the batter.

Turn the batter into the prepared tin. Bake the cake
for about 1¼ hours, until a skewer inserted into the
centre comes out clean.

Loosen the cake from the sides of the tin; turn the
cake out on to a wire rack and remove the lining paper. Turn the cake the right way up and leave it to cool
completely before icing it.

To make the orange topping, beat the curd cheese,
honey and grated orange rind together. Spread the
mixture over the top of the cake and flute it with a
palette knife. Sprinkle the orange julienne round the
edge of the cake.

Pear and Orange
Upside-Down Cake

Serves 10

Working time: about 20 minutes

Total time: about 2 hours and 30 minutes

Calories 160, Protein 2g, Cholesterol 0mg, Total fat 5g,
Saturated fat 0g, Sodium 110mg

2	*pears, peeled and sliced*
1 tsp	*fresh lemon juice*
3	*oranges, peel and pith sliced off*
175 g/6 oz	*brown flour*
3 tsp	*baking powder*
90 g/3 oz	*light brown sugar*
3 tbsp	*safflower oil*
1/2 tsp	*pure vanilla extract*
1 tbsp	*clear honey*
2 tbsp	*fresh orange juice*

Preheat the oven to 170°C (325°F or Mark 3). Grease a 20 cm (8 inch) round sandwich tin. Line its base with greaseproof paper and grease the paper.

Sprinkle the pear slices with lemon juice. Cut two of the oranges into segments, discarding the membranes. From the third orange, cut one slice across the grain of the segments. Put this slice in the middle of the prepared tin. Radiating out from the central slice of orange, arrange alternate orange segments and pear slices to cover the base of the tin.

Sift the flour and baking powder into a bowl, then stir in the sugar. Whisk the oil with the vanilla extract and 15 cl (1/4 pint) of cold water until well blended. Make a well in the centre of the dry ingredients and stir in the oil mixture. Beat well with a wooden spoon until the batter is smooth and glossy.

Pour the batter over the fruit in the tin and level the top with a small palette knife. Bake in the centre of the oven until well risen, lightly browned and springy when touched in the centre—40 to 45 minutes.

Leave the cake in the tin for 5 minutes, then loosen its edge with a palette knife. Turn the cake out of the tin on to a wire rack and remove the lining paper. Leave the cake to cool.

Heat the honey and orange juice gently in a small saucepan, stirring to blend the mixture. Boil the liquid for about 30 seconds until it is syrupy. Quickly brush the oranges and pears with the glaze.

Pear and Port Wine Cheesecake

Serves 12
Working time: about 40 minutes
Total time: about 2 hours and 30 minutes
Calories 200, Protein 4g, Cholesterol 35mg, Total fat 10g, Saturated fat 3g, Sodium 195mg

175 g/6 oz *digestive biscuits, crushed*
60 g/2 oz *unsalted butter, melted*
1 tsp *ground cinnamon*
250 g/8 oz *medium-fat curd cheese*
60 g/2 oz *caster sugar*
1 tsp *finely grated lemon rind*
1 *egg*
3 *large pears*
1 tbsp *fresh lemon juice*
6 tbsp *port*
1 tbsp *currants*
1 tsp *arrowroot*

Preheat the oven to 180°C (350°F or Mark 4). In a bowl, mix the biscuit crumbs with the butter and cinnamon. Spread the mixture over the bottom of a 22 cm (9 inch) round springform cake tin and press lightly. Bake the biscuit base for 15 minutes, then leave it to cool.

With a wooden spoon, beat together the curd cheese, sugar, lemon rind and egg. Peel and core the pears. Slice them thinly and sprinkle the slices with lemon juice. Cover the biscuit base with the cheese mixture, then arrange the pear slices on top in an overlapping pattern. Bake the cheesecake for about 35 minutes until it is set. Leave the cake to cool in the tin, then transfer it to a serving plate.

Put the port, currants and arrowroot in a small pan. Cook them, stirring, over gentle heat for 1 minute, until the liquid thickens. Leave it for a minute or two to cool; spoon the mixture over the cake to glaze the pears.

Petal Ring Cakes

Makes 12 cakes
Working time: about 50 minutes
Total time: about 1 hour and 25 minutes
Per cake: Calories 140, Protein 2g, Cholesterol 60mg,
Total fat 8g, Saturated fat 4g, Sodium 25mg

30 g/1 oz	*caster sugar*
2 tbsp	*kirsch*
1 tbsp	*icing sugar*
12	*sugar-frosted rose petals*
12	*sugar-frosted freesia petals*

Genoese sponge

2	*eggs*
1	*egg white*
60 g/2 oz	*caster sugar*
90 g/3 oz	*plain flour*
15 g/¹/₂ oz	*unsalted butter, melted and cooled*

Kirsch cream filling

1 tsp	*caster sugar*
1 tsp	*kirsch*
15 cl/¹/₄ pint	*double cream*

Preheat the oven to 190°C (375°F or Mark 5). But twelve 7.5 cm (3 inch) dimple moulds, dust them lightly with flour and place them on baking sheets.

Prepare a genoese sponge mixture using the ingredients listed here. Fill each dimple mould almost to the top with sponge mixture and bake them until the sponge is well risen, lightly browned and springy to

the touch—10 to 15 minutes. Carefully unmould the ring cakes on to a wire rack to cool.

Put the 30 g (1 oz) of caster sugar and 2 tablespoons of kirsch in a small non-reactive saucepan with 2 tablespoons of cold water and heat gently. When the sugar has dissolved, boil the syrup rapidly for 1 minute, then remove it from the heat.

Cut each ring cake in half horizontally, keeping matching pairs together, cut sides uppermost. Brush each cut surface with a little of the kirsch syrup.

To make the filling, whisk together the egg white, sugar, kirsch and cream until the mixture will hold a peak. Spoon the filling into a piping bag fitted with 5 mm (¹/₄ inch) star nozzle. Pipe the cream decoratively over the bottom half of each cake, and replace the tops. Sift the icing sugar over the cakes, then pipe a whirl of cream into their centres. Decorate with the sugar-frosted rose and freesia petals.

SUGAR-FROSTED PETALS

Applying a Coating: Beat an egg white until it lightens without foaming. Brush violet, primrose, freesia or rose petals with the white, then dip them in caster sugar. Transfer them to a plate and leave in a warm place until dry and hard In an airtight container, they will keep for weeks.

Pineapple Cake

THE PINEAPPLE MAKES THIS CAKE VERY MOIST. AS A RESULT, THE CURRENTS DO NOT REMAIN DISTRIBUTED THROUGHOUT THE BATTER BUT FORM A LAYER AT THE BOTTOM OF THE CAKE.

Serves 12
Working time: about 25 minutes
Total time: about 3 hours
Calories 220, Protein 4g, Cholesterol 40mg, Total fat 10g, Saturated fat 2g, Sodium 95mg

125 g/4 oz *polyunsaturated margarine*
125 g/4 oz *light brown sugar*
2 *eggs*
200 g/7 oz *plain flour*
1³/₄ tsp *baking powder*
125 g/4 oz *currants*
200 g/7 oz *fresh pineapple flesh*

Preheat the oven to 170°C (325°F or Mark 3). Line a 20 cm (8 inch) round cake tin with greaseproof paper and grease the paper.

Using a wooden spoon, cream the margarine and sugar together until light and fluffy. Beat in the eggs one at a time, following each with 1 tablespoon of the flour. Sift in the remaining flour, together with the baking powder. With a metal spoon or rubber spatula, fold the flour into the batter, then mix in the currants. Purée the pineapple in a food processor or blender, and fold it into the cake mixture.

Turn the mixture into the prepared tin and level the top. Bake the pineapple cake for about 1¹/₄ hours, until it is firm to the touch and golden-brown. Leave the cake in the tin for 10 minutes, then turn it on to a wire rack and leave it to cool. Remove the lining paper.

Pineapple Rondels

Makes 12 rondels
Working time: about 1 hour and 30 minutes
Total time: about 2 hours
Per rondel: Calories 250, Protein 5g, Cholesterol 70mg,
Total fat 6g, Saturated fat 1g, Sodium 35mg

3	*eggs*
1	*egg white*
125 g/4 oz	*vanilla-flavoured caster sugar*
125 g/4 oz	*plain flour*
1	*medium pineapple, skin and eyes removed*
3	*large oranges, skin and pith sliced off*
125 g/4 oz	*granulated sugar*
30 cl/¹/₂ pint	*orange-flavoured pastry cream*
90 g/3 oz	*shelled walnuts, finely chopped*

Preheat the oven to 180°C (350°F or Mark 4). Grease a 38 by 28 by 2 cm (15 by 11 by ³/₄ inch) baking tin and line it with non-stick parchment paper.

To make the sponge bases for the rondels, put the eggs and egg white in a large bowl with the caster sugar. By hand or using an electric mixer, whisk the eggs and sugar for 5 to 6 minutes over a pan of hot, but not boiling, water on a low heat, until it becomes thick and very pale. Remove the bowl from the saucepan and continue whisking until the mixture is cool and will hold a ribbon trail. Sift the flour very lightly over the top of the mixture and carefully fold it in with a metal spoon or a rubber spatula. Pour the batter into the prepared tin and spread it evenly. Bake for 25 to 30 minutes, until the sponge is well risen, lightly browned and springy to the touch.

Turn the sponge on to a large wire rack and loosen the paper but do not remove it. Place another rack on top, then invert the racks together so the paper is underneath: if the sponge rested directly on the rack, it would stick to the metal. Allow the sponge to cool.

Meanwhile, cut the pineapple into 12 equal slices. Remove the hard centre core from each slice with a small plain cutter. Trim the slices into neat rings, using an 8 cm (3¹/₄ inch) cutter as a guide.

Remove the two ends of each orange and slice the remainder crosswise to create four uniform slices. Heat 60 g (2 oz) of the granulated sugar with 15 cl (¹/₄ pint) of water in a wide, shallow pan. When the sugar dissolves, bring the syrup to the boil and simmer for 3 minutes. Poach the pineapple and orange slices, in batches, in the sugar syrup for about 2 minutes— just long enough to soften them slightly. Lift the slices from the syrup with a slotted spoon and transfer them to a wire rack to drain. Boil the remaining syrup to reduce its volume by about half.

Transfer the cooled sponge and its paper to a board. Using an 8 cm (3¹/₄ inch) plain round cutter, cut 12 rounds from the sponge cake. Brush each round with the reduced syrup.

Spread each round of sponge with the orange-flavoured pastry cream, coating the top and sides evenly. Cover the sides only with the chopped walnuts. Lift the rounds off the paper on to a large foil lined baking sheet. Place a slice of pineapple and a slice of orange on each coated sponge round.

To make caramel for a garnish, gently heat the remaining granulated sugar in a small pan with 3 tablespoons of cold water. Stir the syrup and brush the sides of the pan with hot water from time to time. When every granule of sugar has dissolved, bring the syrup to the boil and cook until it turns golden-brown.

Very lightly oil two baking sheets. Allow the caramel to cool slightly, then trickle it in fine lines from a small spoon across the baking sheets. The caramel will set within seconds. Break it in pieces and pile the fragments on top of each cake.

Pistachio Battenburg Cake

THE CHEQUERED BATTENBURG CAKE IS USUALLY COVERED IN ALMOND MARZIPAN; HERE, PISTACHIOS REPLACE ALMONDS, TO GIVE A MARZIPAN WITH AN UNUSUAL FLAVOUR AND A NATURAL GREEN COLOUR.

Serves 16

Working time: about 1 hour

Total time: about 14 hours

Calories 250, Protein 3g, Cholesterol 30mg, Total fat 12g, Saturated fat 2g, Sodium 180mg

125 g/4 oz	*polyunsaturated margarine*
125 g/4 oz	*light brown sugar*
2	*eggs*
175 g/6 oz	*plain flour*
1½ tsp	*baking powder*
2 tsp	*strong black coffee*
1 tsp	*cocoa powder*
3 tbsp	*apricot jam without added sugar*

Pistachio marzipan

175 g/6 oz	*shelled pistachio nuts*
90 g/3 oz	*caster sugar*
90 g/3 oz	*icing sugar*
1 tsp	*fresh lemon juice*
1	*egg white, lightly beaten*

For the pistachio marzipan, blanch the pistachio nuts for 2 minutes in simmering water. Drain them, enfold them in a towel and rub them to loosen their skins. Peel the kernels. Spread them out on kitchen paper for several hours to dry in a warm place.

Preheat the oven to 180°C (350°F or Mark 4). Line a rectangular tin approximately 28 by 18 by 4 cm (11 by 7 by 1½ inches) with non-stick parchment paper, making a deep pleat across the centre to divide the tin crosswise into two portions.

Using a wooden spoon, cream the margarine and brown sugar together in a large bowl until very pale and fluffy. Beat in the eggs one at a time, following each with 1 tablespoon of the flour. Sift the remaining flour and the baking powder together into the mixture and fold them in.

Transfer half of the mixture to a second bowl. Into one portion beat the coffee; into the other, beat the cocoa powder together with 2 teaspoons of water. Spoon the coffee sponge mixture into one side of the prepared tin and the chocolate mixture into the other side. Cook the sponges for 20 to 25 minutes, until they are firm to the touch. Turn them out on to a wire rack, remove the lining paper and leave them to get cold.

Meanwhile, grind the pistachios finely into a bowl, using a rotary grater or a food processor. Add the caster sugar and sift in the icing sugar. Mix in the lemon juice and enough of the beaten egg white to give a firm but pliable consistency.

Trim the sponges to the same size and cut each in half lengthwise. Spread the side of one chocolate sponge lightly with jam and press one of the coffee sponges against it. Join the other two sponges with jam in the same way. Spread jam over the top of one pair of sponges. Press the second pair down on the first, making sure that a coffee sponge is over a chocolate sponge, and a chocolate sponge is over a coffee sponge, so that the cake will have a chequer-board cross section.

Dust the pistachio marzipan with a little icing sugar and roll it out between two sheets of non-stick parchment paper. Remove the top sheet and trim the marzipan into a rectangle just large enough to enclose the sponge—about 30 by 22 cm (12 by 9 inches). Spread all four surfaces of the sponge very lightly with jam and position it in the centre of the marzipan. Wrap the marzipan evenly round the sponge, peeling back the parchment paper. Press the edges of the marzipan together so that they adhere they are very sticky— and trim off the ends.

Stand the Battenburg cake on a serving plate and score the top of the cake with a sharp knife to give a criss-cross pattern. Pinch the top edges with a finger and thumb. Leave the Battenburg cake uncovered overnight; it will become dry enough to slice.

Pumpkin Cake

Serves 16
Working time: about 20 minutes
Total time: about 3 hours
Calories 170, Protein 4g, Cholesterol 15mg, Total fat 9g,
Saturated fat 3g, Sodium 180mg

500 g/1 lb	pumpkin, peeled and chopped
175 g/6 oz	brown flour
3 tsp	baking powder
1 tsp	ground cinnamon
125 g/4 oz	medium oatmeal
60 g/2 oz	light brown sugar
90 g/3 oz	polyunsaturated margarine
1	egg, beaten
Honey-cheese topping	
250 g/8 oz	medium-fat curd cheese
2 tbsp	plain low-fat yoghurt
4 tsp	clear honey
2 tbsp	pumpkin seeds, lightly browned

Preheat the oven to 170°C (325°F or Mark 3). Grease an 18 cm (7 inch) square cake tin. Line the tin with greaseproof paper and grease the paper.

Put the pumpkin in a saucepan with 4 tablespoons of water. Bring the water to the boil and simmer for 2 to 3 minutes, or until the pumpkin is tender. Strain the pumpkin and purée it in a blender or food processor.

You should have at least ¼ litre (8 fl oz) of purée. Leave it to cool.

Sift the flour into a bowl with the baking powder and cinnamon. Add the oatmeal and brown sugar, and stir. Rub in the margarine with the fingertips until the mixture resembles breadcrumbs.

Stir in the egg and ¼ litre (8 fl oz) of the pumpkin purée, then beat the mixture with a wooden spoon for 1 minute until smooth. Spoon the mixture into the tin and level the top with a small palette knife.

Bake the cake in the centre of the oven until risen, golden-brown and springy when touched in the centre—50 to 60 minutes. Turn the cake on to a wire rack and remove the paper Leave to cool completely.

Meanwhile, make the topping Put the curd cheese, yoghurt and honey in a bowl and mix them together with a wooden spoon. Spread the top and sides of the cake evenly with the topping and score it with a fork. Press pumpkin seeds against the sides of the cake.

EDITOR'S NOTE: Use bought pumpkin seeds: those from the centre of the pumpkin would be too damp. To brown the seeds, heat them in a heavy-bottomed pan, shaking constantly, for 1 to 2 minutes until the colour begins to change.

Raisin and Ginger Buttermilk Cake

BUTTERMILK IS A LOW-FAT DAIRY FOOD, TRADITIONALLY PRODUCED AS A BY-PRODUCT OF BUTTER-MAKING BUT NOWADAYS OFTEN SPECIALLY PREPARED BY THICKENING SKIMMED MILK WITH A BACTERIAL CULTURE. THIS FRUIT CAKE IS LEAVENED BY THE CARBON DIOXIDE GAS PRODUCED WHEN THE BICARBONATE OF SODA ENCOUNTERS THE ACID IN THE BUTTERMILK.

Serves 16

Working time: about 30 minutes

Total time: about 5 hours

Calories 220, Protein 3g, Cholesterol 0mg, Total fat 8g, Saturated fat 2g, Sodium 130mg

---

175 g/6 oz	*plain flour*
175 g/6 oz	*wholemeal flour*
1/2 tsp	*ground cinnamon*
1/4 tsp	*ground ginger*
1/4 tsp	*ground mixed spice*
150 g/5 oz	*polyunsaturated margarine*
125 g/4 oz	*light brown sugar*
1	*lemon, grated rind only*
90 g/3 oz	*currants*
90 g/3 oz	*raisins*
60 g/2 oz	*mixed candied peel, chopped*
1/4 litre/8 fl oz	*buttermilk*
1 tbsp	*black treacle*
3/4 tsp	*bicarbonate of soda*

Preheat the oven to 170°C (325°F or Mark 3). Line a 22 by 12 cm (9 by 5 inch) loaf tin with non-stick parchment paper.

Sift the plain flour into a bowl and mix in the wholemeal flour, cinnamon, ginger and mixed spice. Add the margarine and rub it in until the mixture resembles fine breadcrumbs. Mix in the sugar, lemon rind, currants, raisins and peel. Heat the buttermilk gently in a saucepan, then stir in the treacle until it melts. Add the bicarbonate of soda to the pan and stir until it froths. Combine this liquid with the dry ingredients and mix until they are evenly blended.

Turn the mixture into the prepared tin and level the top. Cook the buttermilk cake for about 1 1/4 hours, until it is well risen and firm to the touch; a skewer inserted in the centre should come out clean. Turn the buttermilk cake out on to a wire rack and leave it to cool completely before removing the lining paper.

Saffron Fruit Cake

MORE COMMONLY KNOWN AS A SPICE FOR SAVOURY DISHES, SAFFRON
IS ALSO INCLUDED FOR ITS GOLDEN COLOUR AND DISTINCTIVE AROMA IN
MANY TRADITIONAL CAKES.

Serves 24
Working time: about 25 minutes
Total time: about 4 hours and 30 minutes
Calories 192, Protein 3g, Cholesterol 25mg, Total fat 8g,
Saturated fat 1g, Sodium 75mg

2 tsp	saffron threads
500 g/1 lb	brown flour
4 tsp	baking powder
175 g/6 oz	polyunsaturated margarine
125 g/4 oz	demerara sugar
150 g/5 oz	dried apricots, four reserved, the rest chopped
7	dried figs, three reserved, the rest chopped
2	eggs
60 g/2 oz	icing sugar, sieved

Preheat the oven to 170°C (325°F or Mark 3). Grease a 20 cm (8 inch) square cake tin. Line it with greaseproof paper and grease the paper. Put the saffron threads in a small saucepan with 17.5 cl (6 fl oz) of water and bring the water to the boil. Remove the pan from the heat and leave the saffron liquid to cool.

Sift the flour and baking powder together into a mixing bowl, and rub in the margarine until the mixture resembles breadcrumbs. Stir in the demerara sugar, chopped apricots, chopped figs, eggs, and 15 cl (5 fl oz) of the saffron liquid. Beat the mixture with a wooden spoon for about 1 minute.

Spoon the mixture into the prepared tin and level the top with a small palette knife. Bake the cake in the centre of the oven until risen, golden-brown and springy in the centre 55 to 60 minutes. Leave the cake in the tin to cool for 5 minutes, then turn it out and remove the lining paper. Invert the cake on to a wire rack and leave it until completely cold.

Halve the reserved apricots and slice the reserved figs. Arrange the fruit in a line across the top of the cake. Mix the icing sugar thoroughly with the remaining saffron liquid. Dribble the icing over the cake and fruit. Leave it to set.

EDITOR'S NOTE: The apricots and figs can be replaced by other dried fruits such as prunes, pears and peaches.

Semolina Fruit Cake

Serves 14

Working time: about 30 minutes

Total time: about 4 hours and 30 minutes

Calories 215, Protein 4g, Cholesterol 40mg, Total fat 11g,
Saturated fat 3g, Sodium 120mg

125 g/4 oz	*polyunsaturated margarine*
125 g/4 oz	*soft brown sugar*
2	*eggs*
125 g/4 oz	*semolina*
60 g/2 oz	*plain flour*
1 tsp	*baking powder*
2 tbsp	*skimmed milk*
60 g/2 oz	*mixed candied peel, chopped*
30 g/1 oz	*shelled hazelnuts, toasted and chopped*
125 g/4 oz	*currants*

Almond paste

25 g/³/₄ oz	*icing sugar*
25 g/³/₄ oz	*caster sugar*
45 g/1¹/₂ oz	*ground almonds*
2 tsp	*egg white, lightly whisked*
¹/₂ tsp	*lemon juice*
¹/₂ tsp	*cocoa powder*

Preheat the oven to 180°C (350°F or Mark 4). Line an 18 cm (7 inch) square cake tin with non-stick parchment paper.

Cream the margarine and sugar together until very pale and fluffy. With a wooden spoon, beat in the eggs one at a time, following each with 1 tablespoon of the semolina. Sift the flour with the baking powder and add them to the mixture with the rest of the semolina and the milk. If necessary, add a few drops more milk to give a soft dropping consistency. Fold in the mixed peel, hazelnuts and currants. Turn the mixture into the prepared tin and level the top.

Cook the cake for about 1 hour, until it is firm to the touch and a skewer inserted in the centre comes out clean. Leave the cake in the tin for 5 minutes, then turn it out on to a wire rack. Leave it until cool before removing the lining paper.

To make the almond paste, sift the icing sugar into a bowl and mix in the caster sugar and almonds. Add the egg white and lemon juice. On a board sprinkled with icing sugar, knead the paste lightly until smooth.

Divide the almond paste in half and knead the cocoa into one portion. Roll out the paste into several long cylinders about 5 mm (¹/₄ inch) in diameter. Twist each brown cylinder with a white one to make a rope. Lay strips of almond rope diagonally across the cake at about 4 cm (1¹/₂ inch) intervals and trim the edges off neatly. The almond ropes should stick to the cake by themselves if lightly pressed, but if not, attach them with dabs of honey.

EDITOR'S NOTE: To toast hazelnuts, place them on a baking sheet in a 180°C (350°F or Mark 4) oven for 10 minutes.

Simnel Cake

A SIMNEL CAKE, TRADITIONALLY SERVED AT EASTERTIME, INCLUDES A CENTRAL LAYER OF MARZIPAN BAKED AS PART OF THE CAKE, AND 11 MARZIPAN BALLS ON TOP TO REPRESENT 11 OF JESUS' 12 APOSTLES; JUDAS, THE BETRAYER, IS OMITTED. IN THIS VERSION OF THE CAKE, THE MARZIPAN IS MADE WITH GROUND HAZELNUTS, WHICH CONTAINS LESS FAT THAN THE MORE COMMONLY USED GROUND ALMONDS.

Serves 16
Working time: about 50 minutes
Total time: about 7 hours and 30 minutes
Calories 325, Protein 9g, Cholesterol 40mg, Total fat 4g, Saturated fat 3g, Sodium 75mg

15 cl/¼ pint	*skimmed milk*
15 cl/¼ pint	*fresh orange juice*
60 g/2 oz	*unsalted butter*
175 g/6 oz	*dried apricots, chopped*
175 g/6 oz	*dried dates, chopped*
175 g/6 oz	*dried figs, chopped*
125 g/4 oz	*sultanas*
125 g/4 oz	*raisins*
60 g/2 oz	*currants*
125 g/4 oz	*soya flour*
½ tsp	*ground cinnamon*
½ tsp	*ground cloves*
¼ tsp	*ground allspice*
1 tsp	*grated nutmeg*
175 g/6 oz	*wholemeal flour*
2	*eggs, beaten*
½ tsp	*bicarbonate of soda*
1 tsp	*clear honey*
2 tbsp	*icing sugar*

Hazelnut marzipan

125 g/4 oz	*shelled hazelnuts, ground*
90 g/3 oz	*wholemeal semolina*
125 g/4 oz	*light brown sugar*
½ tsp	*almond extract*
1	*egg white*

Preheat the oven to 140°C (275°F or Mark 1). Grease a deep 18 cm (7 inch) round cake tin. Double-line the tin with greaseproof paper and grease the paper. To protect the outside of the cake from scorching during the long cooking, tie a double thickness of brown paper round the outside of the tin and stand the tin on a baking sheet double-lined with brown paper.

Put the milk, orange juice and butter in a large saucepan. Bring the mixture to the boil. Add the apricots, dates, figs, sultanas, raisins and currants. Stir the fruit well and bring the liquid back to the boil, stirring occasionally. Remove the pan from the heat and leave the fruit to plump up, until it is barely warm.

Meanwhile, make the hazelnut marzipan. Mix the nuts, semolina, sugar and almond extract in a bowl. Add enough of the egg white to form a soft, pliable dough. Knead the marzipan on a lightly floured board until smooth. Cover the board with a large sheet of plastic film. On the plastic film, roll out one third of the marzipan and trim it to an 18 cm (7 inch) round. Set the remaining marzipan aside.

Sift the soya flour into a large bowl with the cinnamon, cloves, allspice and nutmeg. Add the wholemeal flour. When the fruit in the saucepan has cooled, add the eggs and bicarbonate of soda to the pan and stir well. Gradually stir the fruit into the flour mixture with a wooden spoon.

Spoon half of the cake batter into the prepared tin and level the top with a palette knife. Pick up the plastic film with the marzipan round on it and invert the marzipan on to the batter in the tin; spread the remaining cake batter over the marzipan and level the top with a small palette knife.

Bake the cake in the centre of the oven until risen and dark brown—2 to 2½ hours. Test the cake by inserting a warm skewer into its centre. If the skewer is clean when removed, the cake is cooked; otherwise return the cake to the oven and test at 15-minute intervals. Leave the cake to cool in the tin, then turn it out and remove the lining paper.

From the unused marzipan make 11 balls about 2.5 cm (1 inch) in diameter. On the plastic film, roll the remaining marzipan into a round to fit the top of the cake. Brush the top of the cake with the honey and set the marzipan round in position. Flute the edge by pinching it with a thumb and forefinger. Arrange the 11 marzipan balls round the edge of the cake, attaching them with a dab of the honey.

Place the cake on a grill rack. Set it on the grill floor under a moderate grill. To flavour the marzipan and cook the semolina in it, leave the cake under the grill until the marzipan is lightly browned—about 10 minutes. Let the marzipan cool.

Sift the icing sugar into a bowl. Mix in 2 teaspoons of water and beat until the icing is smooth. Pour the icing over the centre of the cake and leave it to set.

EDITOR'S NOTE: For a light-coloured marzipan, use yellow semolina and caster sugar in place of the wholemeal semolina and brown sugar. Three oranges should yield 15 to 20 cl (5 to 7 fl oz) of juice.

Spiced Apricot Balmoral Cake

THIS CAKE IS NAMED AFTER THE RIDGED BALMORAL LOAF TIN IN WHICH IT IS COOKED.

Serves 10

Working time: about 35 minutes

Total time: about 4 hours

Calories 225, Protein 4g, Cholesterol 45mg, Total fat 7g, Saturated fat 4g, Sodium 80mg

200 g/7 oz	*plain flour*
1$\frac{1}{2}$ tsp	*baking powder*
$\frac{1}{2}$ tsp	*grated nutmeg*
60 g/2 oz	*polyunsaturated margarine*
90 g/3 oz	*light brown sugar*
1	*orange, grated rind only*
90 g/3 oz	*dried apricots, finely chopped*
1 tbsp	*black treacle*
4$\frac{1}{2}$ tbsp	*skimmed milk*

Nutmeg buttercream

30 g/1 oz	*unsalted butter*
60 g/2 oz	*icing sugar*
$\frac{1}{8}$ tsp	*grated nutmeg*
	fresh orange juice
7	*dried apricots, halved*

Preheat the oven to 180°C (350°F or Mark 4). Thor-oughly grease a 25 cm (10 inch) Balmoral loaf tin or a 22 by 12 cm (9 by 5 inch) loaf tin.

Sift the flour and baking powder into a bowl and mix in the nutmeg. Add the margarine and rub it in until the mixture resembles fine breadcrumbs. Stir in the sugar, orange rind and chopped apricots. In an-other bowl, whisk together the egg, treacle and skimmed milk; add them to the first bowl and blend the ingredients thoroughly with a wooden spoon.

Turn the mixture into the prepared tin and level the top. Cook the cake for about 50 minutes, until it has risen to the top of the tin; it should be firm to the touch and just beginning to shrink from the sides of the tin. Turn the cake out on to a wire rack and leave it until it has cooled completely.

Meanwhile, make the buttercream. Cream the but-ter until it is soft, then sift in the icing sugar. Add the nutmeg and beat the mixture with a wooden spoon. Add a few drops of orange juice to give a piping con-sistency. Spoon the buttercream into a piping bag fit-ted with a medium-sized star nozzle and pipe a con-tinuous row of shells along the top of the cake. Alter-natively, spoon the buttercream down the length of the cake. Decorate the cake with the apricot halves.

Spiced Teacakes

Makes 12 teacakes
Working time: about 50 minutes
Total time: about 2 hours and 40 minutes
Per teacake: Calories 235, Protein 6g, Cholesterol 30mg,
Total fat 5g, Saturated fat 3g, Sodium 30mg

250 g/8 oz	*plain flour*
¹/₂ tsp	*salt*
¹/₂ tsp	*grated nutmeg*
¹/₄ tsp	*ground cloves*
¹/₂ tsp	*ground cinnamon*
¹/₂ tsp	*groundall spice*
¹/₄ tsp	*ground mace*
250 g/8 oz	*wholemeal flour*
60 g/2 oz	*light brown sugar*
30 g/1 oz	*unsalted butter*
30 g/1 oz	*fresh yeast, or 15 g (¹/₂ oz) dried yeast*
1	*egg, beaten*
6 tbsp	*soured cream*
60 g/2 oz	*currants*
60 g/2 oz	*sultanas*
2 tbsp	*clear honey*

Sift the plain flour, salt and spices into a large bowl. Mix in the wholemeal flour and sugar. Rub the butter into the flours and make a well in the centre of the

mixture. Dissolve the yeast in 15 cl (¹/₄ pint) of tepid water; if using dried yeast, leave it to stand, following the manufacturer's instructions. Pour the yeast liquid into the centre of the flour and add the egg and soured cream. Mix to form a soft dough.

Knead the dough on a lightly floured surface for about 10 minutes, until it is smooth and elastic. Put the dough in a clean bowl. Cover the bowl with plastic film and leave it in a warm place for about 1 hour, until the dough has doubled in size. Meanwhile, butter and lightly flour three baking sheets.

Knock back the risen dough, then knead in the currants and sultanas. Divide the dough into 12 equal pieces. Knead and shape each piece into a smooth ball. Roll them with a rolling pin into flat rounds about 10 cm (4 inches) in diameter and place four on each baking sheet. Prick the rounds well with a fork.

Loosely cover the teacakes with plastic film and leave them in a warm place for about 30 minutes, until doubled in size. Meanwhile, preheat the oven to 220°C (425°F or Mark 7).

Bake the risen teacakes for 15 to 20 minutes, until they are golden-brown and sound hollow when lightly tapped on the base. Remove the teacakes from the oven and immediately brush them with honey. Leave them on wire racks to cool.

Strawberry Shortcake

Serves 10
Working time: about 45 minutes
Total time: about 2 hours and 30 minutes
Calories 220, Protein 5g, Cholesterol 25mg, Total fat 11g,
Saturated fat 4g, Sodium 305mg

150 g/5 oz	*plain flour*
60 g/2 oz	*ground almonds*
3 tbsp	*caster sugar*
1 tbsp	*baking powder*
45 g/1½ oz	*unsalted butter*
5 tbsp	*butter milk*
15 g/½ oz	*flaked almonds*

Strawberry filling

250 g/8 oz	*strawberries, one reserved, the rest hulled and chopped*
4 tbsp	*claret or port*
125 g/4 oz	*cottage cheese, sieved*
4 tbsp	*double cream, whipped*
1 tbsp	*caster sugar*
	icing sugar to decorate

Preheat the oven to 200°C (400°F or Mark 6). Add the chopped strawberries for the filling to the claret and leave them to macerate.

Sift the flour, ground almonds, sugar and baking powder together into a bowl. Rub in the butter until the mixture resembles fine crumbs. Stir in about 4 tablespoons of the buttermilk—enough to give a soft dough. Knead the dough gently on a lightly floured surface, then press it out to an 18 cm (7 inch) round. Place the round on a non-stick baking sheet.

With a knife, mark the top of the dough into 10 sections. Brush the top with buttermilk and sprinkle it with the almonds. Bake the shortcake for about 25 minutes, until it is crisp and golden. Turn it out to cool on a wire rack. When the shortcake is cold, split it in half horizontally and cut the top into the 10 sections.

To make the strawberry filling, mix the cottage cheese with the whipped cream and caster sugar. Strain the juice from the macerated strawberries and keep it for another use; then fold the strawberries into the cream mixture.

Just before serving the cake, spread the strawberry cream over the base of the shortcake. Cover it with the 10 top sections and dust them lightly with icing sugar. Slice the reserved strawberry and arrange the slices in the centre of the cake.

Tropical Fruit Cake

Serves 24
Working time: about 30 minutes
Total time: about 5 hours

Calories 275, Protein 4g, Cholesterol 45mg, Total fat 10g, Saturated fat 3g, Sodium 145mg

250 g/8 oz	*polyunsaturated margarine*
250 g/8 oz	*light brown sugar*
4	*eggs*
350 g/12 oz	*plain flour*
3 tsp	*baking powder*
45 g/1½ oz	*angelica, chopped*
125 g/4 oz	*dried papaya, chopped*
125 g/4 oz	*dried pineapple, chopped*
75 g/2½ oz	*shredded coconut*
60 g/2 oz	*banana chips, crushed*
2 tbsp	*skimmed milk*
1 tbsp	*apricot jam without added sugar*

Preheat the oven to 180°C (350°F or Mark 4). Grease a 22 cm (9 inch) round cake tin and line it with non-stick parchment paper.

Put the margarine, sugar and eggs in a mixing bowl. Sift in the flour and baking powder. Reserve 15 g (1½ oz) of the angelica, 30 g (1 oz) of the dried papaya, 30 g (1 oz) of the dried pineapple and 15 g (½ oz) of the shredded coconut for decoration. Roughly chop the rest of the shredded coconut. Add the remaining angelica, papaya, pineapple and chopped coconut to the bowl, then add the banana chips and the skimmed milk. Mix until the ingredients are thoroughly blended, then beat the batter firmly with a wooden spoon for 2 minutes until it is smooth Turn it into the prepared tin and level the top.

Cook the fruit cake for about 2 hours, until it is well browned and firm to the touch; a skewer inserted in the centre should come out clean.

Cool the cake for 5 minutes in the tin, then turn it out on to a wire rack and leave it to cool completely. Peel off the lining paper. Warm the jam in a small saucepan and brush it over the top of the cake. Sprinkle the top of the cake with the reserved tropical fruits.

Vanilla Angel Cake

ANGEL FOOD CAKE CONTAINS NO FAT AT ALL, AND IS SWEET AND
TOOTHSOME ENOUGH TO BE ENJOYED WITHOUT ICING OR GARNISH.
LEAVENED WITH MANY EGG WHITES, THE CAKE DOUBLES IN SIZE DURING
BAKING; FOR SUCCESS WITH A LARGE ANGEL FOOD CAKE SUCH AS THIS A
TUBE CAKE TIN IS ESSENTIAL, SINCE WITHOUT THE TUBE THE OUTSIDE OF THE
VOLUMINOUS CAKE WOULD DRY OUT BEFORE THE CENTRE HAD SET.

Serves 16
Working time: about 40 minutes
Total time: about 4 hours
Calories 120, Protein 2g, Cholesterol 0mg, Total fat 0g,
Saturated fat 0g, Sodium 30mg

150 g/5 oz	plain flour
150 g/5 oz	icing sugar
10	large egg whites
1 tsp	cream of tartar
1/2 tsp	pure vanilla extract
1/2 tsp	almond extract
175 g/6 oz	caster sugar

Preheat the oven to 190°C (375°F or Mark 5).

Sift the flour and icing sugar together into a bowl.
Put the egg whites, the cream of tartar, vanilla extract
and almond extract in a large, grease-free bowl—

preferably of copper, which reacts chemically with
the egg whites to strengthen the walls of the air bubbles. Using a hand-held electric whisk or, for the copper bowl, a large balloon whisk, whisk the egg whites
until they form soft peaks. Whisk in the caster sugar 1
tablespoon at a time, and continue whisking until the
whites form stiff peaks. Fold in the flour and icing
sugar mixture one quarter at a time. Be careful not to
over-stir the mixture: fold only until the flour disap-
pears into the egg white.

Spoon the batter into an ungreased 25 cm (10 inch)
angel cake tin. Run a knife through the batter to expel
excessively large air bubbles. Bake the angel cake in
the centre of the oven for 40 to 45 minutes, until the
mixture springs back when lightly pressed with a fin-
gertip. Invert the tin on to a wire rack and leave the
cake to stand upside down in its tin for about 2 hours,
until it has cooled completely.

Ease the cake from the side of the tin with a palette
knife; it will then come out easily. Stand the angel
food cake on a serving plate and remove any loose
fragments of the browned sponge from the surface
of the cake before serving.

Vinegar Cake

THE VINEGAR REACTS WITH THE BICARBONATE OF SODA TO RELEASE CARBON DIOXIDE, WHICH LEAVENS THE CAKE. THIS DOES NOT AFFECT THE FLAVOUR.

Serves 20

Working time: about 20 minutes

Total time: about 3 hours and 30 minutes

Calories 220, Protein 2g, Cholesterol 0mg, Total fat 8g, Saturated fat 2g, Sodium 130mg

350 g/12 oz	plain flour
125 g/4 oz	ground rice
1/2 tsp	allspice
175 g/6 oz	polyunsaturated margarine
125 g/4 oz	raisins
125 g/4 oz	sultanas
125 g/4 oz	mixed candied peel
17.5 cl/6 fl oz	milk
3 tbsp	cider vinegar
1 tsp	bicarbonate of soda
90 g/3 oz	icing sugar
1 1/2 tbsp	fresh lemon juice

Preheat the oven to 170°C (325°F or Mark 3). Grease a deep 25 by 11 cm (10 by 4 1/2 inch) oblong tin. Line it with greaseproof paper and grease the paper.

Put the flour, ground rice and allspice into a mixing bowl. Add the margarine and rub it in finely with your fingertips until the mixture resembles breadcrumbs. Stir in the raisins, sultanas and candied peel.

Heat the milk in a saucepan until it is tepid. Stir in the vinegar and bicarbonate of soda, which will froth up. Immediately add the frothy liquid to the fruit mixture in the bowl, so as not to lose too much of the gas. Stir with a wooden spoon to blend the ingredients, then beat them to achieve a smooth, soft consistency. Spoon the mixture into the prepared tin. Level the top with a small palette knife.

Bake the cake in the centre of the oven until well risen, golden-brown and springy when touched in the centre—about 1 hour and 10 minutes. Loosen the edges with a small palette knife, turn the cake out of the tin on to a wire rack and remove the lining paper. Leave the cake until it has cooled completely.

With a wooden spoon, beat the icing sugar with the lemon juice in a small bowl until smooth. Spoon the icing into a greaseproof paper piping bag and pipe a lattice design over the top of the cake. Leave the cake until the icing has set.

Black Cherry Chocolate Gateau

Serves 12

Working time: about 50 minutes

Total time: about 3 hours

Calories 140, Protein 5g, Cholesterol 60mg, Total fat 5g,
Saturated fat 3g, Sodium 80mg

500 g/1 lb *black cherries*
1¹/₂ tsp *powdered gelatine*
3 *eggs*
100 g/3¹/₂ oz *caster sugar*
90 g/3 oz *plain flour*
15 g/¹/₂ oz *cocoa powder*
¹/₂ tsp *baking powder*
3 tbsp *kirsch or brandy*
175 g/6 oz *medium-fat soft cheese*
5 tbsp *whipping cream*
15 g/¹/₂ oz *chocolate curls*

Preheat the oven to 190°C (375°F or Mark 5). Grease a round cake tin about 21 cm (8¹/₂ inches) in diameter and line it with non-stick parchment paper.

Set aside 13 or 14 perfect cherries to decorate the cake. Simmer the rest very gently in 15 cl (¹/₄ pint) of water until they are tender but still intact—7 to 8 minutes. Strain the liquid into a measuring jug and, if necessary, make up the volume to 175 cl (6 fl oz) with water. Put 1 tablespoon of water in a small bowl and stand it in a pan of gently simmering water. Add the

gelatine. When the gelatine has dissolved, stir it into the cherry liquid. Halve the cherries, discarding the stones, and add them to the liquid. Leave the liquid to cool, then refrigerate it until it sets—about 2 hours.

Meanwhile, put the eggs and all but 2 teaspoons of the sugar in a large bowl resting over a pan of hot, but not boiling, water. Whisk by hand or with an electric mixer until the eggs are thick and very pale. Remove the bowl from the heat and continue to whisk until the whisk leaves a heavy trail when lifted. Sift the flour, cocoa and baking powder together twice and fold them quickly and evenly through the egg mixture with a metal spoon. Turn the batter into the prepared tin and level the top. Cook for 20 to 25 minutes, until well risen and firm to the touch. Turn the sponge out on to a wire rack, loosen the lining paper but do not remove it and leave the sponge to cool.

To assemble the gateau, cut the sponge in half horizontally and place the bottom half on a serving plate. Sprinkle it with the kirsch. Mix the soft cheese with the remaining sugar and spread half of it over the sponge. Stir the cherry jelly, and spread it and the stewed cherries evenly over the cheese. Top the cherries with the second layer of sponge. Spread its top with the remaining cheese mixture.

Whip the cream and spoon it into a piping bag fitted with a small star nozzle Pipe a lattice of cream on to the cake. Arrange the chocolate curls and reserved cherries in the gaps Chill the cake until it is served.